The Great Alaskan Dinosaur Adventure

The Great Alaskan Dinosaur Adventure

BUDDY DAVIS
MIKE LISTON
JOHN WHITMORE

Master
Books

First printing: August 1998

ISBN: 0-89051-232-9
Library of Congress Number: 98-66309

Cover by Janell Robertson

Printed in Canada.

Contents

Preface and Acknowledgments

This is a true adventure story about five men who went to the North Slope of Alaska in 1994 in search of frozen, unfossilized dinosaur bones. The primary text of this book was adapted from the journal of John Whitmore, the trip leader. Major additions to the original text were made by Buddy Davis and Mike Liston. We need to thank many for the publication of this book, especially our spouses and families who supported us in prayer while we were in Alaska. Above all, we thank the Lord whose hand was so evident during our journey.

The expedition was funded by private contributions from the team members themselves and from members and friends of the Creation Research Science Education Foundation (CRSEF) of Columbus, Ohio. Cedarville College provided some funds to help with the travel expenses of John Whitmore from the faculty development fund.

Major editorial comments and additions were provided by George Detwiler, Dan Specht, Ken Ham, Jamie Whitmore, and Kay Davis. We are deeply indebted to them for their help. The photographs contained within this volume were contributed by all of the team members. The original drawings were made by team member Buddy Davis.

The expedition team included:

Buddy Davis, Bladensburg, Ohio. Buddy is a dinosaur sculptor, artist, and owner of Wildlife Studios. His sculptures and taxidermy are valuable assets to his position as curator of the Answers in Genesis Creation Museum. He is also a recording artist and tours with Answers in Genesis seminars worldwide. Buddy is an explorer, veteran ark searcher, and has been on numerous dinosaur digs.

George Detwiler, West Liberty, Ohio. George taught science and math at Urbana High School from 1965 to 1995. He is now teaching the same subjects at Calvary Christian School in Bellefontaine, Ohio, where he is free to teach all aspects of biblical creationism. He has a B.S. in chemistry from Wheaton College (IL) and a M.A.T. for science teachers from Michigan State University. He has an Ohio permanent professional teaching certificate covering all major areas of science. He has also taken students on geology/ecology/backpacking/camping trips to the southwestern United States.

Mike Liston, Gambier, Ohio. Mike is president of his own company that designs and makes outdoor and rescue gear. He can best be described as an outdoorsman and explorer. He guides and trains groups for cave exploring and rappelling trips. Mike travels and speaks often at churches, seminars, and television interviews about his creation adventures.

Dan Specht, Westerville, Ohio. Dan is a dentist in Columbus, Ohio, and has been in private practice there since graduating from Ohio State University's dental school in 1961 with a D.D.S. Before that he was in the U.S. Army, Army Security Agency, from 1951 to 1954. He is an experienced white water rafter and has led numerous rafting trips in West Virginia.

John Whitmore, Cedarville, Ohio. John has been teaching geology at Cedarville College since graduating from the Institute for Creation Research in 1991. He has an M.S. in geology from ICR and a B.S. in geology from Kent State University, Kent, Ohio. He speaks frequently in churches and schools on topics related to biblical creationism and geology.

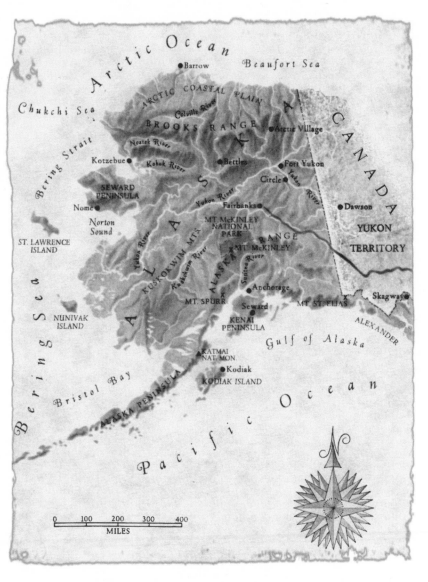

MAP OF ALASKA.

1

North to Alaska

Monday, July 11

Our small bush plane headed north for the land of the midnight sun. Five minutes after leaving Fairbanks, there was nothing but wilderness as far as the eye could see. Our destination: the Colville River, 200 miles north of the Arctic

THE RUGGED BROOKS MOUNTAINS
OF CENTRAL ALASKA.

Circle. The Colville drains the Brooks Mountain range and flows north into the Arctic Ocean.

The pilot crammed the five team members of our expedition and all of the gear we would need to survive in the rugged terrain for two weeks into the tiny plane. We prayed that we had the proper gear for our journey into the unknown. We were going to be out of contact with the rest of the world for two weeks and there was no way of knowing about some of the hardships that we would face — or the many triumphs with which the Lord would bless us. Our Arctic Alaska adventure had begun!

John Whitmore, from Ohio, led the diverse group. George Detwiler was the most experienced outdoorsman of

the group. He also shot the video for the expedition. Buddy
Davis is a veteran explorer of Mt. Ararat, and brought with
him his vast knowledge of dinosaurs. Dr. Dan Specht took
care of our medical needs. He was the only one who had
significant white water rafting experience. Mike Liston provided valuable insights into the equipment, clothing, food,
and gear that we needed for the trip.

After six months of serious planning we were finally
ready to go. Mike and Dan were flying out of Columbus
early in the afternoon. Buddy, George, and John left
Cedarville at 10:30 a.m. for Indianapolis. The flights to
Alaska this time of year were so full that it was impossible
for us to travel on the same flight, although we tried. Under-
standably, most tourists also head to Alaska during midsum-
mer. We started to "pipe dream" about this trip about a year
earlier. Now, it was finally becoming a reality. It had only
been two weeks since we bought our tickets, finalized trans-
portation on the North Slope, and knew for sure that we
could go. Not just anyone can go and excavate these bones.
We had to have permission from the Bureau of Land Man-
agement (B.L.M.) since they are on federal land. The per-
mits came just days before our scheduled departure.

Our destination was the Liscomb Bone Bed on the North
Slope. Frozen, partially fossilized dinosaur bones can be
found in abundance in the coal and shale layers of these
beds. These bones attracted us. Part of the research John
had been conducting involved the chemical analysis of
dinosaur bones. Where could be a better place to collect
pristine, unaltered bones than here? An added attraction of
these bones was their frozen state. If original organic remains
were still left in the bones, the cold temperatures may have
helped preserve them. There are other closer and less remote

areas where dinosaur bones can be found. However, we were after these bones in the hope they would contain organic remains that would support the creation model of earth history.

John, Buddy, and George's flight did not go as planned. For some reason the plane on which we were to fly from Denver to Seattle never arrived in Denver. Of course, this bungled all of the other flights we were supposed to be on from Denver to Seattle to Anchorage, and then on to Fairbanks. We became anxious because we were due to meet Dan and Mike in Seattle and had no way to communicate with them and tell them otherwise. Also, our bush plane was scheduled to leave Fairbanks at 8:00 a.m., and we wondered if we would make it on time. We did manage to make it to Fairbanks after some rerouting and patience by 2:00 a.m., Tuesday morning. (And only two hours late!)

After a 14-hour flight and passing through four time zones, we arrived quite tired. Nevertheless, the flight up the coast of Alaska was unforgettable. As we were flying, we witnessed a beautiful sunrise. It was about 1:30 in the morning! The mountains below were absolutely spectacular. They were snow covered and had glaciers hugging their valleys. Although we were dead tired, we could not sleep. It was a geologist's paradise! Between the clouds, the shoreline could be seen where the mountains and glaciers met the ocean. Just before arriving in Anchorage we could see Denali (Mt. McKinley) which is the highest mountain peak in North America — it dwarfed everything around it.

Tuesday, July 12

Dan and Mike made it to Fairbanks two hours earlier. We had arranged ahead of time to spend the night in the hangar of the bush pilot who was going to fly us north in the morning. The hangar was on the opposite side of the airport from the commercial terminal. Buddy was fascinated with all the mounted Alaskan wildlife near the baggage claim. (Before he started sculpting dinosaurs, he was a taxidermist.) We wondered how much of this wildlife we would see. All three kinds of North American bears live in Alaska (grizzly, black, and polar) and this was one bit of wildlife we did not want to run into unexpectedly. We brought along a twelve-gauge shotgun with slugs and a rifle just in case. After picking up our bags, we hailed a taxi for the four-mile ride around to the other side of the airport. The taxi driver asked where we were from and where we were going. After he found out we were headed to the North Slope, he burst out laughing and said "I hope you guys have some plasma — the mosquitoes are going to eat you alive!" Well, we were in Alaska and we had swatted a few mosquitoes outside at the airport, but they were bearable. We thought this guy must be exaggerating, trying to poke fun at a few Alaskan rookies.

NEAR DISASTER STRIKES ONLY MINUTES AFTER
LAUNCHING OUR BOATS ONTO THE COLVILLE RIVER
FROM UMIAT. MIKE AND GEORGE'S RAFT ALMOST
SANK IN THE COLD, GLACIAL STREAM. MIKE IS PAD-
DLING AND GEORGE IS HOLDING UP THE FAR SIDE TO
KEEP IT FROM SINKING AS THEY ARE BEING SWEPT
ALONG IN THE SWIFT CURRENT.

2

What Did We Get Ourselves Into?

When we arrived at the hangar, Mike and Dan were
already sleeping. It was now 3:00 a.m. and all of the doors
were locked. When we finally pounded hard enough on the

glass office door, we saw a strange figure arise from the floor. It was Mike sleeping in his full mosquito gear! He was wearing his headnet and bugsuit. Mosquitoes were *inside* the hangar! After getting inside, Buddy, George, and John quickly followed suit with their mosquito gear and bedded down for a short night. The mosquitoes weren't bad, but the bug stuff and netting were necessary. If the mosquitoes were no worse than this, we could live with them. Little did we know what was to come!

By the time we got to bed it was already light outside. Since Fairbanks has only a few hours of semi-darkness this time of the year, this would be the last hint of darkness we would see for the next ten days. The sun stays up all night north of the Arctic Circle in the summer. That's where we were headed in a few short hours — the land of the midnight sun.

Though we were very tired, we could not sleep. It must have been a combination of the mosquitoes, light, and anxiety. As we tried to sleep with the smell of "bug stuff" and our mosquito nets over our heads, we wondered what we were about to encounter. John gave up trying to sleep about 5:00 a.m. He was not alone. The others were awake as well. The hot shower in the hangar bathroom that morning would have to last nine days. There would be no modern conveniences, flush toilets, or hot water on the tundra. Our bush plane could carry only 1,500 pounds plus fuel and pilot. This limited us as to what gear we could bring, so we each had to pack judiciously. It felt strange to leave on a camping trip without a flashlight but they wouldn't be needed due to the 24 hours of sunlight. Trying to decide what to take and what to leave behind at the hangar was difficult. It was especially hard when we were dead tired wading among all the gear and bodies. For a while it amounted to mass confusion! There was a large scale, kind of like the ones once used in banks, on which we weighed all of our gear, food, and bodies. Because of Mike's expert advice and our careful packing in the weeks before, we barely came in a few pounds under our 1,500 pound allowance! Dan was even able to take his portable plastic toilet seat — though he received much ribbing from Buddy and Mike.

A man in greasy jeans and t-shirt began to load our gear and prepare the twin engine Navajo Chieftain for the two-and-one-half hour flight at 7:30 a.m. After topping off the fuel tanks and checking the oil, the "mechanic" jumped into the pilot's seat and fired up the engines. He then hollered at the five startled team members, "Let's go!" It was with shock that we realized the "mechanic" was really our bush pilot — and a very good one at that!

Warbelow's Aviation flew us over central Alaska from Fairbanks to Umiat. We left the ground at 8:15. Once our plane was airborne, the city of Fairbanks was quickly swallowed up in the majestic Alaskan wilderness. It was an unusually clear day, according to our pilot. The Brooks Mountains were spectacular. As we traveled north, we found a delightful mix of mountains, tundra, woods, and rivers. We could see the fabled Yukon River and the Alaskan Pipeline. It was worth the trip to Alaska just to ride in the bush plane. The skilled pilot would jockey the small plane around the rugged mountain slopes, pointing out abandoned and working gold mines and searching for big game animals. There were no roads and towns; it was completely barren, desolate, and wild. After crossing the rugged, but not particularly high Brooks Mountains, we had our first glimpse of the North Slope. The terrain was very flat and featureless

UMIAT, WITH THE COLVILLE RIVER IN THE BACKGROUND.

except for the braided and meandering rivers that scarred the landscape along with glacial kettle lakes. It is usually less than three months between snows this far north, so there were no trees, only endless miles of green, grassy tundra.

Many Alaskan bush pilots fly like the old timers — by the seat of their pants. Our pilot told us stories of fatigued pilots who failed to use their instruments and eventually flew their aircraft into the ground. Not many landmarks for reference can be found on the flat and featureless terrain. From the air, the tundra looks very much the same, making this type of flying very hazardous. Getting lost would be very easy. The pilot told us that if you crashed your plane up here the mosquitoes would suck you dry if the crash didn't kill you. We found that kind of hard to believe at first. As Umiat appeared in the distance we could see the Colville River meandering across the landscape. To its west was the beginning of a high bluff that we would follow for most of the 120 miles while on the river. It was in the outcrop of rock along these bluffs where the dinosaur bones would be found. We wondered what the Lord had in store for us in this barren landscape.

About five minutes before landing in Umiat, our pilot reached behind his seat and grabbed his Deep Woods OFF from his flight bag. He began to apply his "bug stuff" liberally. We began to think this was premature until we landed in Umiat on the gravel runway at 10:30 a.m. Suddenly, we were shocked at the swarms of mosquitoes outside the plane. Had we made the right decision about coming this far and being left behind with so many mosquitoes? From our vantage point inside the plane, they sounded like an angry swarm of bees and they were waiting for us to come out so the feeding could begin. We had prepared physically for the mosquitoes with 100% DEET, mosquito headnets, and bug net shirts, but we were not prepared mentally. (Bug shirts are hooded shirts made of mosquito netting with elastic around all the openings.) How in the world could there be this many bugs? The only time during the next nine days we would have a break from the mosquitoes was when the wind would blow harder than ten miles an hour, or while safely in our tents.

We had never seen a pilot work so fast. He had the plane unloaded and was up in the air again within five minutes. He didn't even stick around to say goodbye or let us have a second look in the plane to make sure we had gotten everything. He probably took off so fast to make sure we wouldn't change our minds and go back with him. After the pilot left, we sat around in shock on top of our pile of gear wondering what we were doing in such a desolate place. The DEET kept the mosquitoes from landing on our exposed skin, but we could do nothing about the swarms that constantly enveloped us. Had we made the right decision? Would we ever make it home alive and sane? What had we gotten ourselves into?

Umiat is a strange little ghost town. Its heyday was probably 20 years ago when the oil industry was booming and it created new towns as exploratory wells were drilled. Umiat often shows up in *USA Today* as one of the coldest places during the Alaskan winter. Now, only three people live in Umiat — at the most. O.J. is the town's only permanent resident and self-declared mayor. He is a veteran pilot of

THE UMIAT HILTON.

World War II. When O.J. came walking out of the trailer, he was not wearing a headnet! When we asked him about it, he just said, "Oh, you get used to them after a while." We thought he was absolutely nuts and incredibly tough to put up with the mosquitoes. Little did we know that within a week we would be just the same as O.J.

Bob was also there when we landed, sitting on a picnic table among the mosquitoes. Ray, with whom we had made all of our raft rental arrangements, was in Fairbanks picking up supplies. He had taken one of Umiat's small planes. We never got to meet him. We really expected Umiat to be a little bigger, because it shows up in bold print on most maps of Alaska. The town is full of abandoned trailers that look similar to those you would find on a construction site. Oil companies must have used these as barracks to house their workers and then left them there. The "office" in Umiat consisted of three or four of these trailers connected together. The front of the office had several moose and caribou racks above the door along with a sign that read "UMIAT HILTON, POPULATION: ONE." Large tanks sitting around the buildings contained diesel fuel. This was their energy for the long winter. A fuel plane flies to Umiat every few months to fill them. A satellite telephone is the only way Umiat is connected to the outside world. Umiat sits on the banks of the Colville River. It was here we rented our three small river rafts and began our adventure.

Bob and O.J. do not get away from Umiat very often. They seemed to enjoy talking with us longer than we really wanted. We were anxious to begin our journey. We paid them $1,000 to rent three small rafts, life jackets, and paddles. The rental price included O.J. flying to Nuiqsut to pick them up ten days later. Due to our very limited budget and the high cost of everything in the Arctic, we could only afford the three rafts. We would much rather have flown directly to the dig site in a helicopter. We were going to have to do this the hard way — with rafts and no outboard motors. When we saw our rafts for the first time, the sight of them gave us quite a jolt! They were sitting in a large pile only half-inflated with some patch kits on top. All of the rafts had patches where previous leaks had been. All of the paddles were of different lengths and some were even cracked and split. We paid $1,000 for this!? But this is the Arctic — you can't just run out to the store and get what you need.

While we pumped up the rafts, O.J. gave us some advice about where to camp and what to expect. He said, "Boys, this is a beautiful part of Alaska. When you're camping on the river, try to keep it that way. Stay out of the willows 'cause the grizzlies like it in there. Whatever you do, don't fall in the river. It will kill you within minutes." Bob and O.J. took us down to the river in two old pickup trucks. The only way to get this kind of vehicle this far north is to drive it there in the winter — when the ground is frozen. The trail to the river was bumpy and we crossed several small streams along the way. We must have been quite a sight riding with our fully inflated rafts and gear in the backs of the dilapidated pickups. The Colville is only slightly narrower than the Ohio or Missouri, but probably not as deep. It is a large river draining the entire north side of the Brooks Mountains. It was cold (from snow melt) and very muddy.

After unloading the trucks, we had to decide who would ride in which raft. We had five men and 15 duffel bags to fit into one small raft and two medium rafts. Where do you put all your gear — at one end or in the middle? We didn't have a clue! Adding to the confusion, O.J. threw us a couple of patch kits and said, "One works for the neoprene raft and one for the PVC raft. I don't know which one is which." He also gave us three air pumps. We found out later that only one of them worked. O.J. also told us we could float to our pickup point in the Eskimo village of Nuiqsut in just 24 hours. We were about to prove him woefully wrong.

Dan's expertise at rafting showed when he had the raft he and Buddy were sharing ready to go before the others. They pushed off and immediately were swept downstream by the strong current. So it was quite funny when Dan hollered out, "Which way do we go?" We could tell that O.J. was thinking he would never see us or his rafts again! It was only 15 minutes later that the strong current had carried Buddy and Dan out of sight. John was alone in the small red raft. Mike and George were in the other and they had just pushed off. They really didn't have a chance to settle among their duffels or grab a paddle, since the swift current pushed them along the sheer bank at a dizzying speed. Suddenly, their raft began to sink. Somehow it began losing air, and they didn't know why. They could hear air escaping but with all their duffel bags in the way they could not find the leak. George had to hold up the deflating side of the raft while Mike paddled frantically to get to shore. The current was swift and the ten-foot bank dropped directly into the water preventing them from landing. They were swept along for some distance before they could drag themselves onto a small ledge. The raft nearly sank before they could get to shore. It was only because of God's help that they got to shore before certain catastrophe. After beaching themselves, they discovered that some gear was on top of a valve and apparently had dislodged it, causing the escaping air.

While standing on the narrow, crumbling ledge, one of

them had to hold onto the pitching raft, or it would be swept away. The other pumped it up and rearranged their gear. It was with much hesitation that they got back in and started off again. They were later to find out that their raft had the only working air pump in the group. If one of us had fallen into the river, it is not certain that we could have survived before being taken over by hypothermia. The water was very cold. Mike and George were also very fortunate that they had not lost any of their precious gear. Mike never really trusted that raft again. He rode in a different raft for the remainder of the time — always listening for that foreboding sound of hissing air.

By this time, the rest of the team was spread out on the river, with Buddy and Dan close to a mile downstream. They were wondering what had happened, but we had no way of signaling to each other in case of trouble or if we got separated. This was to hurt us more than once in the days to come. Buddy and Dan decided to pull up on the first available gravel bar so that we could regroup.

While we were stopped we ate lunch and gave thanks that George and Mike had escaped certain tragedy. We wondered how we were going to survive the next nine days. We had already had one close call; what would the river bring us next? If somebody got seriously hurt, we did have an aircraft radio with which we could communicate with any planes that flew overhead, but we hadn't seen any. Eating quietly, we contemplated what might happen in the days to come. We had to put our complete trust in the Lord. The Lord alone had supplied the necessary funding for our trip, had allowed us to obtain the necessary permit, and was completely in control of our circumstances. Knowing the Lord would provide gave us a true feeling of peace.

Each of us brought 28 MRE's (meals ready to eat) along for food. These are the same meals used by the military. There were 12 different menus from which to choose. Each package contained a complete self-contained meal, including a main course, crackers, cheese, jelly or peanut butter, candy, dried fruit or desert, fruit drink, chocolate drink, coffee, matches, toilet paper, gum, silverware, and a wet wipe. The meals had more than enough food in them. They were pre-cooked and could be eaten hot or cold. To heat them, the package simply had to be placed in boiling water. Additionally, the meals were completely sealed (so we wouldn't have problems with bears and other animals smelling them). All of

EVERY TIME WE HEATED WATER FOR OUR MRE's, MOSQUITOES WOULD FLOCK TOWARD THE HEAT AND END UP IN THE WATER. IT WAS IMPOSSIBLE TO HEAT WATER WITHOUT MAKING "MOSQUITO TEA."

the trash was completely combustible (no dishes to wash). Although we were tired of MRE's by the end of our trip, they were definitely the best food some of us ever had while in the wilderness. Some of us planned the particular meal they were going to eat, but some chose to be surprised. When meal time came, they just reached into their duffel bag and ate whatever they grabbed hold of. We tried once to have hot chocolate and coffee, but heating water without making mosquito tea first was impossible. The mosquitoes are attracted to the heat, and one could always count on a dozen or so ending up in the drink before it was boiling. The main courses included spaghetti, sliced ham, chicken and rice, tuna and noodles, and pork and rice.

While the others were eating, Mike got out the G.P.S. (Global Positioning Satellite System). This is a small hand-held unit that works by satellite signals to tell you your position (latitude and longitude). It is supposed to work anywhere in the world. Mike was having trouble getting it to accept the coordinates O.J. had provided for the distributary channel leading from the Colville River to our pickup point at Nuiqsut. This was important because there was only one correct channel from the Colville and all the others ended in the Arctic Ocean. After we had finished lunch and gathered our scattered wits, we pushed on down the river.

The river probably flowed several miles an hour along most stretches. There were several areas with muddy rapids and shallow water. Still, for the most part we could drift comfortably along without too much paddling. In a few places we had to get out and pull our boats over some shallow rapids when we could not get into the main current. We wanted to make as much distance on the river as we could, because the bone sites were still far downstream. (The

THE MANY CHANNELS OF THE COLVILLE RIVER NEAR
UMIAT. PARTS OF THE COLVILLE ARE WHAT GEOLO-
GISTS CALL A "BRAIDED" STREAM, WHERE THE STREAM
IS NOT CONFINED TO A SINGLE CHANNEL, BUT FLOWS
THROUGH MANY INTERTWINING CHANNELS. WE OFTEN
BECAME SEPARATED FROM ONE ANOTHER IN THE
MAZE OF CHANNELS.

Colville flows from south to north and ends in the Arctic
Ocean.) As we drifted, we saw occasional rubble tumbling
down the 150-foot bluff on our left and observed the falcons, which nested near the top of the bluff, soaring high
above.

Mike took the opportunity during the easy rafting to
continue working on the G.P.S., but had no luck. The G.P.S.
wouldn't accept the coordinates back at Umiat and he was
still having trouble getting them entered. He had written all
of the coordinates down on a piece of scrap paper, but they

THE MOSQUITOES LOVED MIKE'S BLACK SWEATSHIRT. WE HAD TO WEAR HEADNETS, GLOVES, AND WOOL CLOTHING TO PROTECT OURSELVES FROM THE BUGS.

wouldn't do us any good without the G.P.S. working correctly. When the breeze picked up, the mosquitoes would take cover down inside the raft. When the breeze died, they were back in the air hovering about us. If we wanted to send a few mosquitoes on their way, all we had to do was whack the raft a few times with the paddle when the wind was blowing. This would jar them loose and they would blow away in the wind. We spent the remainder of the day floating with the current and doing some occasional paddling. We thought to ourselves that if the rest of the trip goes this way, it wouldn't be so bad.

Most of the clothing we had brought was for cold weather, but with the 24 hours of sunlight it got quite hot during that first day on the river. Everyone needed to wear a heavy wool shirt and pants. In addition, we all wore headnets and hats to keep the mosquitoes from biting through. We sat quietly and suffered in the heat.

As evening approached, we decided to make camp on a high sand and gravel bar about 9:00 p.m. Fourteen miles were covered on the river. That wasn't bad for the first day. The mosquitoes seemed to get worse and it was getting colder. The temperature for most of the day had been about 70 to 75 degrees (F). When we stopped to camp, the usual routine was to drag the rafts up on the beach and put the paddles and pumps under them. Then we piled rocks on top of the boats and tied the bowline to bushes or rocks. We would not want to lose a boat or two during the night by an unexpected rise in the river. Then we hauled our gear to where camp was to be set up.

We were glad to finally get our tents up. It seemed like it took an eternity because of the swarms of mosquitoes among the small willow bushes next to the river. They were beginning to drive us crazy. Never in our worst nightmares did we think they would be this bad. While setting up our tents we realized a potential problem: How do we get into their tent without taking all of the mosquitoes in with us? We began a ritual that worked, for the most part. We would run around as fast as we could, trying to leave all the mosquitoes behind. Then we would open our tent zipper as quickly as possible and slide into the tent through the smallest possible opening. The next 15 to 20 minutes would be spent killing mosquitoes that had followed us into the tent. After all this, we were finally in a mosquito-free zone! We thought we would have trouble sleeping because there was no darkness. Yet, after the long plane ride, two hours of sleep the night before, and riding in the raft all day, we dozed off quickly — thus bringing to an end a long first day in the wild Alaskan tundra.

A GRIZZLY BEAR LOOKING OVER THE TOP
OF THE WILLOWS.

3

Mosquitoes and the
Ziploc Bag

Wednesday, July 13

All of us were up and eating breakfast by 6:30. Though it was colder (65 degrees F), the mosquitoes were still swarming as hungrily as ever. We set off at 7:30, wondering what the day would bring. As we drifted downstream, we began to see some wildlife. We saw a moose standing in the river up to his shoulders. He didn't do much, but stand and watch our approach. He was not afraid of us and didn't leave until we were within 75 yards of him. By the end of the day we had seen five moose and a caribou.

During the morning we encountered some anxious times. The river often split into many different channels with long islands between. Buddy and Dan went down one channel and George, Mike, and John went down another channel with the other two rafts. Everyone tried to follow Buddy and Dan, but the current was just too strong and we all became separated. After traveling downstream and drifting by several large adjoining channels, we didn't know whether Buddy and Dan were ahead or behind. We began to worry that we would not see them again. The river channels became a maze and trying to choose which one would rejoin the main river was only a guess. All Dan and Buddy could do was raft with the main current and wait and pray! George, John, and Mike debated whether to wait or press hurriedly ahead. Finally, one hour later, we reunited downstream. When we first saw Dan and Buddy, Buddy was waving his arms. We thought he was glad to see us, but it turned out he was trying to get our attention to show us a large bull caribou feeding by the river. It was by God's grace that we found each other so quickly. We were determined never to become separated again. However, this became an impossible task because of the many different currents and channels in the river.

Mike was finally able to get the G.P.S. working while floating on the river. He had to do a complete memory wipe and start programming from scratch. He was very nervous about doing this, as no one else was familiar with it and our lives could very well depend on him being able to run it. At home in Ohio it had taken him two days to program it, using the inch thick manual. Now, floating on a river in the Arctic, he was under tremendous pressure to get it right. As a tribute to the other team members' character, they never bothered Mike or asked him about it. They just left him in peace to work it out.

At many places along the river, the current picked up sand from the bottom of the stream. Occasionally the sand would swirl against the bottoms of our rafts making something like a hissing sound. This made all of us nervous because of the close call we had the day before as we began our journey. Every time we would hear "the noise," we would check all the valves and make sure none were leaking air. We didn't want to do any swimming in the Colville.

As lunch time approached, we came upon a three-mile sand and gravel bar. It was reported in the scientific literature that a dinosaur horn core had been found in the float (loose rock material) near here. We had made good mileage that morning so we ate lunch on the east side of the river, planning to spend part of the afternoon walking the bar looking for fossils. The bar was on the east side of the river, the one hundred foot bluff on the west side.

Buddy was not feeling well; he was sick to his stomach and felt like he had the flu. All he could do that morning was lie in the raft with his eyes closed and try to ignore the rocking of the waves and the mosquitoes that tormented him. Sometimes the river would get too rough for Buddy's partner Dan to handle by himself. He would be forced to ask Buddy to paddle just long enough to get them into calmer water. John was hoping to make more time, but he also needed a healthy crew. He decided that we should pitch our tents and make camp on this island gravel bar following lunch. We had traveled 12-1/2 miles already. The team decided to set up Buddy's tent for him. He felt guilty about having someone do his work for him, but he was too sick and we were a team. If it were one of the others who were sick, Buddy would have done the same for them.

The remainder of the afternoon was spent relaxing. We needed it. We still had not fully recovered from the plane flight and our lack of sleep the ptrvious nights. It was especially enjoyable because the wind was blowing too hard for the mosquitoes. We could take our headnets off for the first time and see Alaska without looking through mosquito netting filters. We found several pieces of fossilized and coalified wood on the bar contained within a hard, tan siltstone matrix. John was hoping to get over to the bluff, but the current was too strong to get over and back. Besides, it looked dangerous because the bluff was very steep and we would

A MOOSE STANDING QUIETLY ALONG THE RIVER'S EDGE.

occasionally see rock falls tumble down the slope and into the river. We were content searching the bar for fossil material.

Not much was seen of Buddy that evening. He was sacked out in his tent trying to get better and was trying to hide from the others just how ill he really was. Toward evening, Dan, George, and John took a walk to the far end of the sand bar. There they saw a pair of moose. Moose have to be the most awkward looking animals one will ever see. They have extremely long legs for their body size. We were able to get rather close to them before they took off running. Moose can be dangerous animals. Cows protecting their calves have been known to fight grizzly bears. Bull moose during the rut are very temperamental and dangerous and have been known to kill people.

As evening approached it began to drizzle and the mosquitoes came back out. Before the other team members turned in that evening, they were standing around and joking about eating mosquitoes along with their evening MRE meal. Buddy could hear them from inside his tent talking about "Kentucky-fried mosquitoes" and he became even more nauseous. Once inside your tent, you do not want to come out until morning because of the mosquitoes. Besides, it was raining.

What does one do if you have to go to the bathroom during the night? George said he had faced that dilemma the night before in our mosquito plagued camp and had used a Ziploc bag in his tent. The rest of us thought this was a good idea, and tried it for the first time. Hey, it's better than going out in the mosquito-infested rain!

BUDDY PULLS THE DINOSAUR JAWBONE INTO THE RAFT.

4

The Eighty-Pound Dinosaur Jaw

Thursday, July 14

It was noticeably colder this morning and the sky was overcast. It stopped raining about midnight but that familiar hum was still outside the tents. The cooler weather and the early hour didn't seem to bother the mosquitoes. Everyone could hear the others rustling around in their tents, packing gear. We didn't see each other until everything in our tents was packed and we were ready to go out and drop our tents.

MIKE WITH THE G.P.S. ALONG THE BANK OF THE
COLVILLE RIVER. THE LISCOMB DINOSAUR BONE BEDS
ARE IN THE BACKGROUND.

Most mornings we even ate inside our tents. We'd ask the
first man out for a mosquito report. It was always bad. Buddy
was feeling much better and we got an 8:00 start hoping to
find some dinosaur bones. We drifted down the river at a
very good pace of 4-5 mph, seeing an occasional moose
standing motionless in the water along the river edge.

We checked our speed with the G.P.S. (global positioning system). The G.P.S. works by receiving signals from at
least 12 of 24 special globe-circling satellites. We could
check our speed, location, and distance to and from certain
points with this instrument. However, as Mike knows, modern technology can fail at any moment. Another piece of
equipment to bite the dust, (literally) was our water purifier
pump. Our only source of water was the muddy Colville

River, and it was so silty it looked like chocolate milk. We had brought along extra filters for the purifier, but they were all hopelessly plugged. We were forced to fill our canteens directly from the river. Fortunately we had iodine tablets to add to the water to kill the germs. Yet they don't filter out the silt and every time we took a drink, we could feel the grit between our teeth!

We were surprised to see a small plane land on a gravel bar about a half mile downstream from us. We didn't expect to see a soul while on the river. As far as we could tell, two people were using binoculars and they were looking at something on the bluff face. Maybe they were studying the falcons; we never found out. They took off as we approached them. We were not even sure if they had seen us. They were flying a small Piper Cub with very large "tundra tires." Apparently, these planes are ideal for Alaska because they do not need much room to land and take off and they can do it at relatively slow speeds. He made a half dozen passes or so before he landed on the bar, probably to make sure it was sufficient for a landing strip.

We had brought an aircraft frequency walkie-talkie with us to be used in case of an emergency. We thought this might be a good time to try it out. But after several failed attempts to contact the plane, we gave up. We found out later that half the bush planes in Alaska don't even have radios!

Our lunch break was near the confluence of the Kikak River. We carefully checked some gravel bars there for dinosaur bones. Some had been reported there in the past. After no success on the bar, we began to work our way over toward the bluff hoping to find something there. John's eyes were peeled to the ground as we worked our way through the willow bushes to the bluff. Suddenly he stopped — as he stared at the ground he saw bear tracks. Worse yet, he saw some smaller tracks — bear cubs. O.J. had warned us about grizzlies in the willows.

Mother grizzlies with cubs are probably the most dangerous North American mammals, besides the polar bear. The willows (small spindly bushes about head high) were thick enough that we couldn't have seen a sleeping sow and her cubs 20 feet away. We were hoping not to surprise a bear. If the bear hears you coming well enough in advance, it will usually leave the area and you alone. But just in case, John sent Buddy and Mike back to the rafts for the twelve-gauge shotgun and the rifle. After checking the bluff out thoroughly, no bone material was found (and better yet, no bears).

FRESH GRIZZLY BEAR TRACKS ALONG THE RIVER'S EDGE NEAR THE WILLOW BUSHES.

BUDDY ON "BEAR WATCH" ON TOP OF THE 150' BLUFF.

Disappointed, we floated down the river a little further hoping to find a camp. It was Mike's turn not to be feeling well. He had a migraine headache due to working on the G.P.S. the first two days. As we drifted along we tried to follow the bluff as closely as possible. Sometimes the current would carry us away from the bluff and we would have to paddle back. We had to be careful not to get too close because of frequent, small, rock falls along the steep bank. The bluff consisted of poorly cemented sandstones and shales that crumbled easily.

John's eyes were especially trained for the hard, tan siltstone that occasionally appeared along the bank. We had found fossil wood in this material the day before on the gravel bar. We stopped several places along the bluff collecting fossil wood and looking for dinosaur material. As of yet, we had not found any bone material on the trip.

Mike was ahead of George and John about 50 yards. Buddy and Dan were behind them, about the same distance. Then John saw it. The current carried George and John swiftly past; they couldn't get to shore for at least another 100 yards. John yelled back to Buddy and Dan to see if they could look at the tan rock he had spotted six inches from the water line with black coloring in it.

They paddled hard, and the instant they were going to pass it by, Buddy reached out of the raft and hauled the 80-pound specimen into the boat. It's a miracle that the heavy fossil did not tear a hole through the raft when Buddy dropped it onto the fabric bottom. He motioned that we should stop. We were barely able to pull over about 100 yards down-

THE LAMBEOSAURUS JAW.

LAMBEOSAURUS, THE LARGEST KIND OF
DUCKBILLED DINOSAUR KNOWN.

stream. Although we were close to shore, it was a struggle to get there because of the swift current very close to the bank.

The specimen Buddy hauled into the boat turned out to be the jaw of a duckbilled dinosaur we have temporarily identified as *Lambeosaurus*. Others had suspected this dinosaur should be present in Alaska, but until our find, the skull bones have never been found to prove it. It turns out the jaw we found is twice the size of any dinosaur jaw yet found in Alaska. From our estimate, this jaw represents an animal at least 40 feet long.

A jaw this large was surprising to us, because most of the previously reported Alaskan bone material has been from juvenile dinosaurs. *Lambeosaurus* is the largest of several kinds of duckbilled dinosaurs.

We were very excited after finding our first bit of bone material. We stopped our boats and prepared to walk along the bank back upstream! Looking carefully, we checked to see if any more bones were present. The current was moving fast along the edge, and the cold, muddy water was certainly over our heads. As always, when we stopped, we gingerly stepped out of the boats. Yet this time the bank gave way underneath Mike and he went in nearly to his waist in water and mud. Jumping out of the water, he immediately changed into his only other set of dry clothes. It was a wake up call for all of us to take our time and be careful.

As we walked back upstream, we found several other large pieces of bone (we think they were limb bones from the same animal) and some additional fossil wood specimens. The large pieces of tan siltstone containing the bones had weathered out of the bank behind us. Who knows how much of the *Lambeosaurus* had rolled down the bank and ended up in the bottom of the river. We were all praising the Lord that we had been allowed to find something so amazing!

After collecting everything we could find, we loaded the rafts and went a short distance downstream to set up camp. We had traveled 13-1/2 miles. This was our most beautiful camp so far. The sand and gravel bar had sparse willows and many kinds of wildflowers.

Our camp was set up in the midst of the wonderful aroma. Our body odor was very bad by this time, so the flowers were extra special. We set up our tents and all had an afternoon nap. As the mosquitoes flew around, they tapped on the tent walls trying to get into our tents. It sounded like

GEORGE BESIDE HIS TENT AT THE "WILDFLOWER" CAMP. THIS WAS A SMALL ISLAND JUST DOWNSTREAM FROM OUR LAMBEOSAURUS DISCOVERY.

rain. Relaxing in our cool bug-proof shelters was absolutely delightful as we smelled the wild flowers. Because it was warm, most of us stripped down to our underwear.

John decided to do a little laundry. The Colville River water may have gotten his clothes dirtier. He even tried to take a bath, but could not go in any deeper than his knees. The water was just too cold. He washed as fast as he could, not only because of the cold water, but the mosquitoes swarmed around his exposed body, biting viciously. He quickly headed for his tent after one of the fastest baths in history!

By 10:00 p.m., everyone was in their tents. The sun was still high in the sky, and it was warm. It must have been

70 or 75 degrees (F). At night we would lie in our tents and wait for it to get dark and for the mosquitoes to quit. However, neither happened. While lying in our tents we could hear a variety of sounds in the background. One of them was the hum of mosquitoes. Another was Buddy and Dan bashing (and smearing) mosquitoes against the sides of their tents.

Every ten minutes or so, some rubble from the bluff, slid downslope, sometimes ending in the river below. This was a frequent sound next to the cliffs. Our camp was situated on a large island, with a small channel of the river separating us from the bluff. The muddy rapids could be

A TRICERATOPS. PROBABLE TRICERATOPS HORN CORES HAVE BEEN FOUND IN ALASKA.

heard churning in the background.

The other bits of wildlife we constantly heard against the background of mosquitoes were the falcons that nested high on the bluff faces. They made small nest holes in steep places on the upper part of the cliff. As they swooped near the crest of the bluff they often made cries, not like an eagle or hawk, but similar to a baby kitten. George was quietly singing praises to our mighty Creator. Thinking back over the day, it had been absolutely amazing. Thanks Lord, for your perfect timing and giving us the privilege to do your work.

JOHN, WAITING THE DUST STORM OUT
ON THE GRAVEL BEACH.

5

Mosquitoes — Rare, Medium, or Well-done

Friday, July 15

As we got up this morning, we were hoping to make good miles toward Ocean Point. Ocean Point is the closest marked map location to the Liscomb Bone Bed. It is about 8 miles or so down river from the bed. We were looking forward to the main goal of collecting from this rich site. Last night, Dan had been relaxing along the river's edge reading a book on his toilet seat. (He was using it for a chair.) While enjoying the evening and filling his canteen he noticed a slight rise in the river. Because of this, he decided to move all of our rafts, paddles, and life jackets to higher ground. It was God's providence that he noticed this, because the river rose one or two feet overnight and became extremely muddy. He dragged the rafts about 4 feet farther up on the beach all by himself, and still, by morning, the back half of the rafts were floating in the water. Dan saved us from what would have been a disastrous situation. If he had not noticed, our rafts would have been far downstream by breakfast. We saw God's hand at work not only in this, but in allowing us to find the jawbone along the river's edge the day before. The jaw was close enough to the river's edge that it would have been underwater if we had floated by one day later. Thanks again, Lord, for your perfect timing!

As we traveled down the river that morning, we made excellent time. The current was moving faster because of the increased amount of water. What would God do next? How could anything surpass the events of yesterday? For the most part, the rocks along the bluff had been horizontally bedded. The rocks consisted of loosely cemented sandstones, shales, occasionally siltstones, and coal beds. As we traveled that morning we encountered some tremendous folds and faults, highlighted by coal beds. We had not expected this after all of the "boring" horizontal stratigraphy we had seen. While floating along photographing folds, faults, and occasionally stopping to get a closer look at some of the rocks along the bluff, we began to hear tremendous noises in the distance. Mike was the first to hear them. We wondered whether someone was shooting a gun or cannon. As

THE ROCK FALLS. THE CLIFF WAS 150' HIGH. SOME
ROCKS AS BIG AS CARS FELL THE FULL HEIGHT OF THE
CLIFF. THE FALLS WERE CONTINUOUS — ONE HAPPEN-
ING SOMEWHERE ALONG THE ONE-HALF MILE CLIFF AT
ALL TIMES. THE STRONG RIVER CURRENT NEARLY TOOK
US UNDER THE FALLING ROCKS.

we rounded a large bend, to our amazement and alarm, we
began to see what was happening.

Ahead of us, on our left, was a sheer cliff approximately
150 feet high and one-half mile long. The strongest current
of the river was pulling us toward the cliff, as it did most of
the time. We were alarmed. In front of us we could see the
cliff giving away, producing massive rock falls that were
crashing into the water below. This is what we had been
hearing for the last half-hour upstream. We began to paddle
furiously, steering the boats to our right to get out of the

main current on our left. Floating along the edge of this cliff would have meant certain death. The rock falls were so continuous and large we would have either been sunk by rocks falling in our boats or capsized by the waves produced from the rocks hitting the water. Finally, after 20 minutes of hard paddling, we made it to a gravel bar across the river from the falls.

Exhausted, we dragged the boats up to the beach and watched in utter astonishment from our vantage point a quarter-mile away. It was like watching fireworks. One didn't know where the next big one was going to happen. The rockfalls were continuous, one happening somewhere along the cliff at all times. Some boulders would plunge the full height of the cliff, landing in the water and creating splashes 20 feet high or more. The falls were the result of a combination of processes and factors. First, as we had already seen upstream, the bluff was inherently unstable. Small falls and slides had already been witnessed. The rocks making up the bluff crumbled very easily. Secondly, the strongest current of the river was at the base of the bluff, undercutting it and causing tremendous amounts of erosion. The river was carrying away every bit of talus building up at the cliff base. The bottom of the bluff simply could not build out. This created the sheer nature of the cliff. Thirdly, the warm sun was melting permafrost at the top of the cliff and creating muddy waterfalls that flowed over the edge of the tundra and into the river below. We suspect this was the catalyst and lubricant that was making the falls so continuous.

This was one of the most amazing geologic spectacles we had ever seen. It was geology in motion. Watching along the half-mile cliff base, no one point could be observed for more than ten seconds without at least one rock falling into the water. Watching the incredible degradation of the cliff before our eyes, we wondered how long this process could continue until the cliff would disappear. How long has this landscape been in existence? Twenty-five years? One hundred years? Could it last one thousand years? Could this process occur for hundreds of thousands of years? The cliff disintegrating before our eyes was direct evidence for a young age of the cliff, the river, and the earth. There was just no other reasonable way to explain why the cliff was still there and had not completely eroded away.

Relaxing and eating our lunch in this special geologic paradise, we could take our headnets off because the mosquitoes were forced to take cover from the wind. What a blessing! Mike was taking the opportunity to dry his pants and socks. The sunshine and wind worked well. Earlier in the day at one of our many stops to look for bone fragments, the bank had given away again and in he went. It was solid one minute then gone the next, eroded away just like the bluff we were watching. After some exploring we found clear water in a small pond. It was found in the middle of the large sand bar on which we were beached. The water purifier had become clogged with silt and was not working, so we were keeping our eyes open for good drinking water. All of our water had to be treated with iodine tablets from here on out. Although the muddy Colville water was drinkable after treatment, it wasn't very appetizing. We would much rather drink water that was clear enough so one could see through to the bottom of their plastic water bottle — and it didn't have that gritty aftertaste. The trouble with iodine tablets is that the water has a nasty iodine taste. We soon learned to sweeten the iodine with powdered drink mixes from our MRE's. Buddy and Mike were getting anxious to head on down the river while the weather was still on our side. Weather conditions could change rapidly, making rafting difficult.

Reluctantly we left our geological paradise, looking over our shoulders for a final glimpse of the spectacular falls. The distant booms continued for an hour as we floated away. Soon the river began to split into many channels. We wanted to stay on the west side of the river, but the wind became stronger than the current, and we ended up in the eastern channels, much to our dismay. Also, we were in danger of being split up again by the many currents and channels. No progress was made down river. Occasionally, it was faster and less tiring to get out of our boats and pull them along the beach instead of trying to paddle. Finally, we were forced to pull over and wait for the wind to die down. Mike tried to get a position fix with the G.P.S., but was not able to get it. We eventually found out that as we got closer to the North Pole the G.P.S. didn't always work as well. It must have been due to the lack of satellites that far north.

As close as we could figure, we were more than two miles away from the bluff in one of the side channels of the river. We really needed to get back closer to the bluff. With the wind blowing there was no need for our headnets. The sky was mostly clear with few cumulus cotton balls, the temperature about 70 degrees (F). The weather on the north slope had been unexpected. We were prepared for much cooler temperatures and more frequent rain. It had only rained once so far; what a blessing.

After a short nap, John went up the beach and into a small meadow among the willow bushes to go to the bathroom. One tries to wait for times when the wind is blowing so your blood loss from mosquito bites on your backside would be reduced. Well, John found out where all the mosquitoes go when the wind is blowing — they take cover in the willows! He exposed as little skin as possible and finished quickly. He got by with a half dozen bites or so. The mosquitoes there don't mess around either. Ohio mosquitoes take their time landing and in selecting the most tender spot. The larger Alaskan mosquitoes land, bite, and are gone in five seconds. You usually don't feel them until it is too late.

The Alaskan tundra has no trees. The largest plant life is the small willow bushes, no higher than your head. They like to grow next to rivers and in low areas near a ravine or stream. Mostly, the tundra is covered with grasses and a half-dozen different types of wildflowers. Seeing these dainty wildflowers growing in this harsh environment reminded us of the writings in Luke 12:27: "Consider the lilies how they grow; they toil not, they spin not; and yet I say unto you, that Solomon in all his glory was not arrayed like one of these." Even in this desolate place, God decorated the landscape. One flower we didn't expect to see north of the Arctic Circle was the dandelion. They are not prolific, but they were there, strong and healthy. We were disappointed to find somebody's trash in this little clearing among the willows. There were several tin cans (one was Spam), beer cans, and other bits of waste. This wasn't the only time we came across trash. We were angry that anyone would spoil the pristine Alaskan tundra like this.

Soon, the wind died down some and our two-hour forced wait was over. Paddling for a long time, and sometimes having to get out and pull the rafts, we were still fighting the wind. We passed through the main channel and made it into one of the western channels. We weren't quite sure where we were on the map. Apparently the channels in this part of the river change so much that it is difficult to keep the maps updated. Our G.P.S. helped, but the coordinates it gave us didn't quite match with the map (it didn't always give an accurate reading). Extremely tired, and yet still wanting to make more progress toward Ocean Point, we stopped and had dinner about 7:30 on a sand bar. We ate quickly and began to talk about trying to make it to the bone beds that evening. However, the Lord had other plans.

Anxious to go, we looked down river. Our hearts sank as off in the distance a large cloud of dust became visible. As we watched, it was getting closer to us. Five minutes later, we were engulfed in a giant dust storm. The wind nearly knocked us over as it hit. The temperature dropped from about 80 degrees down to 45 degrees in 30 seconds, with 40 to 50 mph wind gusts. We certainly didn't expect this, north of the Arctic Circle. For the most part the tundra is soggy and damp, not dry and dusty. The ground freezes down to 20 feet or more in the winter. Only the top two feet or so of the ground thaws when summer comes. Not being able to penetrate into the ground because of the permafrost, the water sits around in small lakes and puddles (ideal for mosquito breeding). However, the tundra does not receive much precipitation. Technically, it could be considered a desert. Where water can drain (along the high bluffs and the sand bars), it can become very dry and dusty. As we got closer to the ocean, the river was getting bigger and it was getting windier and dustier.

We would have to wait the dust storm out. The river became dangerously choppy. The wind was so strong it created white caps (or should we say brown caps, because of the muddy water) nearly a foot high blowing upstream against the current. It would have been life-threatening for us to try to go further. In 1985 John was in the Grand Canyon with George. They will never forget standing next to the fearsome, rushing Colorado River. They say that the Colorado is "too thick to drink and too thin to plow." Looking at the Colville River reminded John of that time next to the Colorado. The wind continued to be strong. After waiting several hours for it to die down, we gave up and dragged our boats across a small channel to set up camp. It took teamwork to set our tents up so the wind did not blow them away. We didn't know why the Lord had stopped us, but maybe we would understand in the morning. Even with all the delays, we made excellent time. It was our best so far with a total of 21-1/2 miles traveled.

At 11:12 p.m., the wind was still blowing, but not as hard. The mosquitoes disappeared for about an hour during the dust storm. Our tents sat back about 15 feet from the river's edge, the doors looking out onto the river, which was about a half-mile wide. There were some small islands out in the middle. Our tents were in a high water channel. One wouldn't want to be here during the spring floods! In front of our tents, along the river's edge, it was very muddy. The ground was so spongy that it would quiver as we walked across. To our back was a thicket of willows where millions of poor little starving mosquitoes lived. They wouldn't get any sustenance from us!

We were learning to tolerate the mosquitoes. They were the most bothersome when we were eating. Ideally, we liked to take our headnets off when eating, but sometimes it was just not possible. John's wife had made his net the night before he left. It didn't look as attractive as the other guys' store-bought nets and Mike's professionally made net. John was slightly embarrassed to have it at first. Then he discovered his net was big enough that he could get both of his hands and his MRE packet into it while eating! John's headnet became the envy of all.

When it came time to eat, George and Dan would take turns using their small backpack stoves to heat up our MREs. The heat of the warm food attracted the mosquitoes. When one would tear open the pouch they were going to eat, the mosquitoes would land right on your food. If peanut butter and crackers were on the menu, just when you spread on the

JOHN, EATING AN MRE INSIDE OF
HIS MOSQUITO HEADNET.

peanut butter they would land and become stuck in it. At the beginning of the journey we would very carefully pick the bugs out, but this wasted food and we had a very limited supply. By the middle of our journey we would look into our open food pouch with disgust at the mosquitoes crawling inside. So, with resignation, we would jam in our spoon and smash them all up. We would tell ourselves that at least they would be dead when they were eaten. By the end of our journey we couldn't have cared less. We would just shovel the food into our mouths, live mosquitoes and all. Food was just something we ate to keep our bodies going, and the little bit of extra protein was not hurting us.

Perhaps we would find some more dinosaur bones tomorrow. We prayed that the Lord would help us be successful again. Maybe we would make it to the Liscomb Bone Bed, the dinosaur locality for which we had come.

GETTING READY TO LEAVE CAMP ON A
COLD, FOGGY MORNING.

6

Out on a Limb —
"Branchiosaurus"

Saturday, July 16

We got an early start, not knowing why the Lord had delayed us from going further the day before. We traveled slowly, carefully checking out the west side of the bank and bluff for bones. About 10:00, Buddy and Dan pulled over on a large sand and gravel bar along the base of the bluff. Would we have passed this island if we were in a hurry to get down the river the night before and had not been stopped by the dust storm? Probably.

The site turned out to be very fruitful. Mike and John both found two bones each in the bar gravel. They were all unfossilized and good-sized. John's not sure if they were dinosaurian. When collecting bones from the stream gravel, there is a possibility one may occasionally turn up some mastodon or mammoth bones that are also to be found on the North Slope. The bones that were found were very muddy, and only small portions of them were sticking out of the mud. Since we found four bones relatively quickly, we thought more would probably be present.

All of a sudden, Buddy became very excited. He had also found something in the mud. As he began to clear the mud and sand away, we thought he had found a long limb bone. His enthusiasm increased as he dug deeper and deeper. George was sent back to the rafts to get the video camera to document this find. As Buddy cleared the sand away, the shape began to look somewhat funny. Mike jokingly said, "Wouldn't it be awful if this were just a piece of wood!" Buddy's heart began to sink as he said, "Maybe that's what it is." It was too good to be true. Buddy was digging out a piece of drift wood! All of the excitement was for naught. All of us were disappointed, but no one more than Buddy. We felt sorry for him. Later, we joked with him a little bit, and we called it his "Branchiosaurus." We ribbed him about his discovery for the rest of the trip.

We formed a row and walked the gravel bar and steep bluff several times searching diligently for more fossil material. No additional specimens were found. The bones

BUDDY, LOOKING OVER HIS "BRANCHIOSAURUS"
IN THE SAND.

didn't appear to be coming from the bluff rocks. They were probably washed here from somewhere upstream. Seeing the fossil bones when one is wearing a headnet is very difficult. The sunshine hitting the netting produces a glare that makes seeing extremely hard. Some team members complained of headaches from the eye strain. The view from the top of the bluff was fantastic. We could see the Colville winding up and downstream for about ten miles in each direction. Dozens of small lakes dotted the landscape. From up there the river no longer looked brown, but was a beautiful deep blue. The sky was clear and the temperature was warm again. A small stream flowed off the tundra down to the gravel bar. The water was clear and we took the opportunity to fill our canteens. We weren't the only ones who used this small stream as a watering hole. There were well-worn animal trails in all directions leading to the stream. Tracks from nearly all types of tundra animals could be found (moose, caribou, wolf, marmot, bear, and goose, to name a few).

The dust continued from yesterday. There is quite a bit of *loess* in Alaska. This is a fine silty substance produced by the scouring action of glaciers. It is sometimes called rock flour and is responsible for most of the dust and grit up there. The dust was as fine as talcum powder and worked its way into everything, including our cameras and guns. It even seemed to blow through the tent walls and settle on everything inside the tents. The dust was another surprise of the North Slope.

Rejoicing in our finds and the beautiful sunny weather, we had lunch before starting downstream again. We should have started sooner, because the further north we went the stronger the wind was getting and the harder the river became to maneuver. Like yesterday, there were several times we had to get out of our boats and drag them along the beach. Our small, inflatable river rafts were no match for the wind and the Colville River. We were constantly buffeted around and blown into the beach. Trying to pull the rafts through the river was a challenge. Our heavy boots, the weight of our gear in the rafts, and the weight of the water on our legs proved exhausting. Finally, we stopped and waited for the wind to die down on a narrow, grass-covered high beach between the river and the bluff. We took the opportunity to eat a cold but bug-free dinner. By 7:00 p.m. we'd been grounded four hours. We really wanted to make it to the bone bed, but it looked like it would have to wait until the next day. We finally continued our struggle, pulling and paddling for another two miles before being stranded up against the bluff, with no beach this time. By 9:00 p.m. the wind was only getting worse and we were getting chilled.

Again, we were stopped for the night because of wind. We only made a pitiful 5 miles on the river. Seeing no place to set up camp where we were stranded, we had to risk crossing the rough river to a sand and gravel bar on the opposite

BUDDY AND DAN. DEAD TIRED WITH MILES TO GO.

side. Everyone put on their life jackets for the dangerous crossing. Fortunately, we didn't lose anyone or any of our precious gear. After we had camp set up, the wind was still blowing and the mosquitoes were forced to take cover. We took advantage of the ideal circumstances and got into our birthday suits. We had our Saturday night bath (whether we needed it or not!). The water was so cold it took our breath away, so the bath didn't last long. It didn't do much good either because the river was quite muddy, but it felt good to get several days worth of sweat and bug stuff washed off. The wind and the sun acted like a giant blow dryer and we hardly had to dry off. By 11:30 p.m. clouds and fog started to roll in, and the temperature dropped down close to the thirties. This was more like the Arctic weather we had expected and it didn't take long for us to seek out the shelter of our tents and the warmth of our sleeping bags.

DAN, CAUGHT UNEXPECTEDLY IN QUICKSAND.

7

Disaster Strikes — Quicksand!

Sunday, July 17

    The wind continued to blow all night without a break. It woke us up several times. At 12:30 a.m. it was light out, but it was an eerie light. The sun was shining at 3:00 a.m. Sleeping with the wind causing our tents to flap in the breeze was hard. A cold front moved in, with fog rising off the river in the morning. (This meant the river was warmer than the air!) With the strong north wind, we hadn't had to wear nets since 3:00 the day before. Sand and silt were everywhere — in our tents, duffel bags, sleeping bags, and clothes. We could not do much about it because of the wind. The water level continued to drop from when it rose Thursday. It went down another six to eight inches during the night, and it looked a little cleaner as well. We were hoping to have a short raft ride as we were only ten miles or so from the Liscomb Bone Bed.

We were wondering if we could make it. By 10:30 a.m., the conditions were no better. This was the type of weather that could ground the expedition for days. John was forced to decide to push on over the objections of some team members. The wind out of the north was still strong, so we decided to tie all three of the rafts together like a train. All five of us then got in the lead raft to paddle. We paddled about three miles and picked up a good river current along the way. The weather was quite foggy and cold — quite a change from yesterday. The weather on the North Slope changes fast, and without warning. We were all dressed in our cold weather and rain gear just to try to stay warm.

About 11:30 we stopped on a sand bar and took some pictures with the eerie, foggy river in the background. It was a much-needed break from a difficult morning of constant paddling and pulling the rafts along the shore. If we didn't keep paddling in the lead raft, the wind would shove the two trailing rafts loaded with gear, up against us. Sometimes they would get around us and there we would be, our three-raft train floating broadside and out of control down the river.

About 1:00 we stopped and had lunch in a small inlet. It was tough getting into because the strong current pushed us by the entrance. We had to beach the rafts and drag them upstream to the inlet. The bank was very muddy and slippery. Finally we decided only some of us could stay in the rafts and the others would pull them. Once we were in the inlet, the water was calm and we paddled to the shoreline. Five miles off in the distance we could see a large bend in the river with the bluff in the background. This was where the Liscomb Bone Bed was. It felt great to finally be able to see our destination.

We saw plenty of animal tracks at our lunch site including a very large grizzly, moose, caribou, and wolf. After lunch, we took a five-mile hike along part of the bluff that did not have river access. We used two rafts to get the five of us across the inlet. A few strokes of the paddle and we were across. We wanted to check the bluff and a gravel bar back upstream for bones.

During the hike we had to cross part of the tundra. Though we were 15 or more feet above river level, we could not avoid stagnant water — which was a great mosquito breeding area. There were many mosquitoes, but they had to stay close to the ground because of the wind. It wasn't easy walking across the tundra. In some places it was like a swamp (called muskeg). We had to put on our heavy hip waders to get across. John found one dinosaur bone fragment on the gravel bar. Flowing through the bar was a relatively clear stream. We filled our canteens with fresh water. When we filled, we always had to remember to drop in an iodine tablet or two and wait at least 30 minutes before drinking.

BUDDY, FILLING HIS CANTEEN FROM THE STREAM. IT WAS DIFFICULT TO FIND STREAMS LIKE THIS THAT HAD "FRESH" WATER. THE COLVILLE RIVER WAS MUDDY AND BROWN.

Consequently, our water didn't taste too good, but none of us got sick from bad water.

Many peregrine falcons nested on the cliff near here. They were very beautiful as they soared high above the bluffs in front of their nests. This kind of falcon is endangered, and is protected by the government. These bluffs along the Colville River are one of the few places that they live.

Buddy and Mike kept their guns ready in case we mistakenly startled a bear and provoked an attack. We tried to make noise to warn our furry friends of our presence. Since Buddy and Mike had the guns, they were the first to go through the thick willows.

Buddy and John walked back across the tundra the way the five of us had come. Dan, George, and Mike walked back to the boats via a small stream channel. This channel probably carries a significant part of the Colville during the spring floods, but it had very little water in it on this day. On their way back they found an old boat motor that someone had abandoned. Whoever it belonged to must have gotten upset with it, because there was a bullet hole in it! Obviously, it had broken down and left someone stranded. Buddy and John found some old barrels. Alaska is no longer unspoiled. It was disappointing to find other people's trash. We also found the skeletal remains of a caribou. Its bones were bleached by the 24-hour days of summer Alaskan sun. Scavengers had scattered some of the bones.

We all met back at our inlet about an hour later. John, George, and Buddy took the opportunity to climb a small bluff so that George could videotape John documenting the bluffs of the Liscomb Bone Bed. The bluffs could be seen approximately five miles downstream. We figured we would be there in about an hour and set camp up, right? Wrong.

The next few miles would be the toughest miles on the river to this point. The north wind was still blowing strongly, and the water was swift and choppy.

In some places we could make good progress because of the current, but in other places the wind was so strong we had to pull our boats along the bluff. This was difficult, because there was just a narrow beach (really a ledge one or two feet wide) of loose material steeply slanting toward the river that had fallen from the bluff above us. The water was very deep here. One slip and we would be in trouble. We kept our life jackets on not only for extra warmth, but because we easily could have fallen into the swift, cold current. The north wind was so strong it was creating one-foot

DRAGGING OUR RAFTS ALONG THE BEACH WAS SOMETIMES EASIER THAN ROWING THEM. THE QUICKSAND WAS AHEAD ON THE LEFT.

waves that were moving *upstream*. It was like riding a roller coaster, and it seemed as though ocean waves were buffeting our small boats. However, we were determined to get to our destination. At 6:00 we arrived at the south end of a two-mile sand and gravel bar. The Liscomb Bone Bed was just past the north end of the bar. Although good camp sites were on the south end, John made what he thought was a good decision — to move on and try to set up camp closer to the bone bed.

It took nearly an hour to pull our boats to the far end of the bar. The wind was probably gusting to 40 miles an hour. Spray began blowing off the river and we could see fog rolling in from the north. The temperature was probably 45 degrees (F), and falling. No telling what the wind chill factor must have been. Paddling the boats was impossible because the wind kept blowing us to shore in the shallow water along the edge of the bar. Although we had on hip boots and rain pants, water was still able to slosh over the top of our boots. Soon, our legs and feet were wet because our boots were full of water. Dan was walking along the beach checking for a campsite. Mike, Buddy, George, and John were paddling the boats across a very shallow mucky bay. The water was only 6 to 12 inches deep and we had to take the boats out further in the river. The bottoms of the boats would drag in the mud, especially Buddy and Dan's, which had the 80-pound dinosaur jaw in the bottom (it was wrapped in a life jacket and plastic tarp). Suddenly, disaster struck! Dan sank up to his knees in quicksand and couldn't get out. He tried, but when he pulled one foot out, it came out without his boot. He frantically waved his arms to signal the rest of the team of his dilemma. However, the rest of the team was headed downstream.

As we turned around and came back upstream to help Dan, Mike was the first to try and reach him. Wading into shore from his raft, he became fast in the quicksand also. It was a terrible feeling to look into Dan's eyes, only 20 feet away, and know that he couldn't be reached. Mike had carried two paddles from his raft. He threw one to Dan and with the other he was able to lie down across it (in the cold water) and pull himself loose from the grip of the quicksand. Mike struggled and succeeded in backing away. He wasn't in as deep as Dan. Mike was soaking wet, but at least he was free of the quicksand. The quicksand was a muddy mixture of sand that was several feet deep. We had always envisioned quicksand as just "wet" sand but the Alaskan quicksand was not like that at all. The muck may have been deposited by the high but slowing moving water in the days before. Mike suggested that Dan lay down and roll out, but he refused.

We didn't know what to do. It was at least 50 feet to solid ground from where he was standing. We had no idea how he got in so far. We couldn't send anybody in after him because then we'd have two people stuck. The wind was blowing and it was getting colder, with a few flakes of snow in the air. Dan was exhausted, wet, and cold. He was beginning to get hypothermic. Complicating matters, the river began to drop. We had even more trouble maneuvering the rafts along the edge of the shallow, muddy-bottomed river. We decided the only way to get him out was to empty one raft and slide in on top of the mud to him. Emptying the raft of our gear allowed the raft to float a little higher in the water. It also made it lighter to pull and shove. The water was only about three inches deep, so we couldn't paddle. It took Buddy and John about 20 minutes to get to him, be-

BY WORKING THE EMPTY RAFT TO DAN, BUDDY
AND JOHN WERE EVENTUALLY ABLE TO FREE HIM
FROM THE QUICKSAND.

cause they kept getting stuck as well, but it worked. Every
time one of them got stuck, they flopped back into the raft.
When pulling the raft any farther was impossible, they sat
on the edge and shoved with their feet, all the while inching
closer to Dan.

Buddy tried getting out of the raft and making contact
with Dan. He had to keep his feet moving continuously.

When he would feel a hint of suction on his feet, he instantly pulled them out to avoid getting stuck in the mucky quick-sand. After a short time (which seemed like an eternity), they were able to stretch a paddle to Dan. Eventually Buddy made hand contact with him. Several times Buddy had to let go of Dan's grip as he started to get stuck himself. Unable to get Dan out, Buddy had to get back in the raft. Again, John and Buddy sat on the edge of their raft and pushed the raft a few feet closer to Dan. Finally they shoved the raft up against the back of Dan's legs and he was able to flop into the boat by himself. John reached down into the mud and pulled his boot out. It took another 20 minutes or so to get back out of the mud into deeper water. We all were cold, but we were especially worried about Dan. He had been standing rela-tively still, absorbing the full force of the foggy damp wind for over an hour.

After getting ourselves and our boats out of the mire, we had to pull them about a mile back upstream to a good campsite. It took about an hour. Dan walked and helped pull. This helped him warm up a little bit, or at least kept him from going deeper into hypothermia. Still, he was shaking from the cold. Buddy's hip boots had water in them and the extra weight was causing his hip joints to hurt. Everyone's clothing was wet or damp, but no one complained. All of our efforts were focused on saving Dan. It was ironic that we needed to administer first aid to our doctor, who was in charge of all the medical supplies. We found a place about two hundred yards from the river in the middle of a sand bar. We carried some gear to the site and made a group ef-fort to get Dan bedded down. Mike and John put up his tent and Buddy brought his gear to the site. Meanwhile, George made some hot food and drink. Mike put Dan into a space

blanket and sleeping bag as soon as possible. When someone is hypothermic, getting them warm as soon as possible
is critical. The food and hot drink helped him considerably.
Mike and John continued putting up tents after we got Dan
bedded down. Buddy carried gear to the campsite and George
continued to cook for all of us. We were all shivering and
close to hypothermia. We appreciated getting into our warm
sleeping bags with hot meals in our stomachs at 10:30. All
of us were exhausted. At least the wind had been blowing
hard enough that evening that we didn't have to put up with
the mosquitoes.

Without a doubt, the Lord was on our side. It seemed
like He allowed us to get into an impossible situation so that
He could provide and take care of us. He surely deserves all
the glory. If we have learned anything, we learned we can
depend on the Lord no matter what the circumstances. We
know people had been praying for us, probably even in the
Sunday night services just before our hour of need. Thanks,
Lord. You are an awesome God!

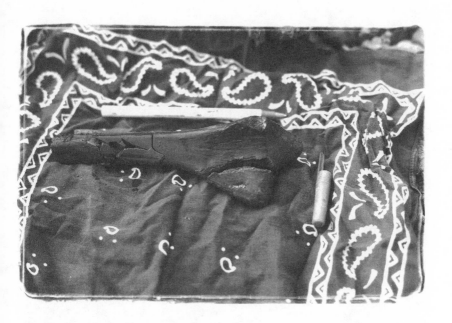

ONE OF THE MANY LIMB BONES WE FOUND FROZEN IN
THE PERMAFROST. MOST OF THE BONES WERE DISAR-
TICULATED AND WERE FROM JUVENILE ANIMALS.
MOST ARE THOUGHT TO HAVE BEEN FROM THE
DUCKBILLED DINOSAUR EDMONTOSAURUS.

8

Dinosaur Bones —
Frozen in Time

Monday, July 18

The fog that rolled in with the cold north wind off the
Arctic Ocean lasted all night. At 8:00 the sky appeared to be

cloudy, and the temperature was about 40 degrees (F). We had waited a long time for this day. We had endured many struggles and hardships to finally make it to this point. We rejoiced in the Lord that yesterday was over and everything turned out well. Before we left, we thanked the Lord for a new day. We had a very relaxing morning. No one was up early because of our hard day the day before and the cool

THE TWO-MILE ISLAND WHERE WE CAMPED FOR THREE NIGHTS (JULY 17, 18, 19) WHILE WE COLLECTED DINO- SAUR BONES. THIS PICTURE WAS TAKEN LOOKING DOWNSTREAM, TO THE NORTH. THE BONE BEDS ARE ON THE FAR HORIZON. DAN GOT STUCK IN THE QUICKSAND ALONG THE FAR RIGHT-HAND SIDE OF THE ISLAND. WE CAMPED IN THE CENTER OF THE ISLAND. FROM THIS VIEWPOINT ON THE BLUFF, OUR TENTS WERE INVISIBLE. THE BLUFF WAS ABOUT 100 FEET HIGH.

morning temperatures. Some of us just didn't want to get out of our nice warm sacks. Besides, Sunday had been anything but a day of rest. After getting up, most of us did a little wash. We had some really muddy clothes from being in the river and in the quicksand. The sun tried to poke through the clouds a few times. The wind died down and a few of the mosquitoes came back. Obviously, the river continued to fall as evidenced by the wide and wet muddy areas exposed on the beaches. After lunch we hiked down to see if we could find some bones.

About 1:00 we began our two-mile hike to the bone site. We were careful to avoid the quicksand Dan was stuck in the night before. We certainly didn't want to go through that ordeal again! When we came to a place that looked questionable, we sent one guy on ahead to test out the mud. Getting stuck was better for one guy than for all of us at once. In fact, Dan did get stuck again, but this time he was able to work his way out. The weather cleared up and the skies were partly to mostly sunny. Large grizzly tracks were in the willows along the way. They looked fresh. We were surprised we hadn't seen a bear. We hoped that when they heard us coming, they'd take off and avoid us. Taking no chances, Buddy and Mike both carried their guns in case of attack.

We easily found the Liscomb Bone Bed. Mike had become very proficient with the G.P.S. and he led us right to it. Before the trip we had received coordinates from someone who had collected at the site previously. There were scattered bits of bone in the rubble above the bed. After removal of the rubble, we found the bones were coming from two coal layers and a gray shale layer sandwiched between. We were digging on a steep slope 15 feet above the river. We could not believe how many bones were present! Most of

the bones we found were disarticulated (they were not lying next to each other in their original life positions). Because of this and the abundance of bones, one is led to believe these are the bones from many animals, not just one or two. Most have been identified as coming from the Hadrosauridae family (known as duckbill dinosaurs). What kind of water catastrophe occurred to deposit these bones from all these animals? Noah's flood? Or perhaps these were post-flood deposits occurring before or after the Ice Age.

When vertebrate animals die, other animals usually scavenge them. Bacteria also play their role, and in a matter

COLLECTING BONES AT THE BONE BED. WE DUG
DOWN SEVERAL FEET THROUGH COAL AND SHALE
TO FIND THE FROZEN BONES. SOME WERE
PETRIFIED, AND OTHERS WERE LIGHTWEIGHT
SHOWING LITTLE PETRIFICATION.

of years (or less) there are no remaining traces of the organism if it dies on land. By far, land would be the normal place for a land animal to die. For example, there were millions of buffalo that roamed the prairies of North America 150 years ago. Where are all of their skeletons today? They have long since disappeared because of the decay process. If something does not happen to a skeleton to prevent decay, it will never become fossilized. The dinosaur bones we found were the result of water deposition. Dinosaurs were land animals. How did their abundant remains end up in water-laid deposits? One hypothesis is that the dinosaurs drowned during

Noah's flood. Their dead, decaying bodies then bloated and floated in the flood waters. As decay progressed, parts of their bodies would fall to the sea bottom and be buried (preventing further decay) by the sedimentary processes of the flood. This is a possible explanation for finding the usual occurrence of partial and disarticulated dinosaur skeletons in water-laid deposits. The bones of the Liscomb Bone Bed seem consistent with this hypothesis. It was interesting to note that modern marine "seashells" occurred in the sediments immediately above the bone beds. There was no obvious non-conformity (erosional surface) between the rocks containing the dinosaurs and these "seashells." This suggested the shells were deposited soon after the dinosaurs and not millions of years later as a conventional view would teach.

The Liscomb Bone Bed has produced the most important dinosaur remains from Alaska. We collected bones on and below the surface. We found both fossilized and what appeared to be *unfossilized* bones. After digging down about three feet, we found more bones frozen in permafrost. We were seeking the frozen unfossilized bones for our research, although we collected some fossilized bones as well. Both types were found together. (We are not sure how to explain it.) One can tell right away whether a bone is fossilized or not because of its weight. The fossilized bones have had minerals deposited within the pore spaces of the bone making them heavier. Within two hours we had plenty of bones for our project. We were surprised at their abundance. John thought we might have needed several days to collect the bones we would need. The Lord was good — He provided everything we found. All the struggles we endured were worth it. After collecting, we had a prayer of thanksgiving and praise for our wonderful Creator. We could not help but praise the Lord for His goodness to us. As we hiked back to camp we wondered how important the bones might be that we were carrying on our backs. What would they contain? Could they help us answer some questions concerning the creation/evolution issue? Only time would tell.

It takes much faith to believe these bones might be 70 million years old. We cannot even imagine how long a million years would be. In the past there may have been countless freezes and thaws that had the potential to destroy the bones. As we were digging we saw the sun melt the ice around the bones and watched some of them turning into a sawdust-like powder. Other bones came out in perfect condition. The older the bones, the more potential they have for being destroyed. The fact that some bones are found in pristine condition may suggest that they are

The duckbilled dinosaur Edmontosaurus. It is believed that most of the bones that occur in the Liscomb bone bed belong to juveniles of this dinosaur.

not millions of years old. It is our belief that these dinosaurs lived only thousands of years ago, and have not been buried for millions of years.

From an evolutionary point of view, approximately 65 million years separates the time these bones were buried and the time of the Ice Age. It is amazing these bones refused to decay and/or become fossilized before they were frozen — if one believes that millions of years existed. Compared to the faith of the creationist, the faith of the evolutionist certainly is incredible. Henry Morris wrote (*Impact* #111, September 1982): "But the faith of the evolutionist and humanist is of another order altogether. His is a splendid faith indeed, a faith not dependent on anything so mundane as evidence or logic, but rather a faith strong in its childlike trust, relying wholly on omniscient Chance and omnipotent Matter to produce the complex systems and mighty energies of the universe."

Perhaps dinosaurs lived alongside man. If one leaves out the evolutionary bias of time we can look at Scripture and see what it says. Any child would come to the conclusion that dinosaurs, along with the other land animals, were created on the sixth day of creation (Gen. 1:24-31). The large creatures described in the Old Testament Book of Job (chapters 40 and 41) fit the descriptions of large dinosaurs and extinct marine reptiles that Job had seen. We do not believe there was a gap or a previous fallen world when the dinosaurs lived. Exodus 20:11 confirms this: "For in six days the Lord made the heavens and the earth, the sea, and all that is in them, but he rested on the seventh day."

It certainly seemed like the enemy had done everything possible to discourage us from getting to the bones. We had been put through the fire with mosquitoes, hypothermia, quicksand, and exhaustion. Our MRE dinner was delicious that night!

We were surprised to see two boats today. Both were heading upstream at full throttle. We saw one while we were digging at the bone bed and another at dinner. We didn't expect to see any civilization up here. After dinner, some of us went over to a quiet part along the edge of the river to wash up. The water was too cold to take a full bath. John tried to wash his hair, but the ice-cold water gave him a headache when he poured it over his head. It was the same feeling one gets when they eat or drink something that is too cold too fast. At 10:00, we headed to bed, again rejoicing in the day's events.

WE ENCOUNTERED A PLAYFUL RED FOX ON THE TUN-
DRA WHO DIDN'T SEEM THE LEAST BIT SCARED OF US.

9

More Mosquitoes, and the Melted Toilet Seat

Tuesday, July 19

We all got up about 8:30 a.m. It was another cold and foggy morning. The weather closer to the ocean seemed different from that farther upstream. The air temperature was 45 degrees (F). John woke up once during the night at 1:30 a.m. and thought it was morning — until he looked at his watch! The sun was brightly shining into his tent from the north. The sun up here circles the horizon during the day. One really can't tell directions from looking at the sun unless they know it gets lower in the sky to the west and north at "night." It won't be long before they start having a few hours of night. By the first day of fall in September, they will be having 12 hours of night (like everywhere else on earth on that day).

After breakfast, we got a few things organized around our tents. Sorting out and drying gear was everyone's favorite pastime. After a week on the river, almost everything had gotten wet or damp. Our duffel bags always went in the bottom of the rafts first because there was nowhere else for them. We usually sat on them so that we were not sitting in the water that collected in the bottoms of the rafts. We enjoyed camping in one place for a few days. Tonight would be the third night we had been here. Tomorrow we would begin our trip toward Nuiqsut. It is a small Eskimo village about 10 miles from the ocean on the Colville River where we would meet our pilot late Friday afternoon. We still had 35 miles of river to conquer, so we planned to get an early start in the morning. Just before lunch John organized all of the dinosaur bones into numbered packages for the trip home. Each person would be responsible for taking one full, two-gallon Ziploc bag with them. They weighed about 30 pounds each. We would have the same weight limits on us during our flight back to Fairbanks so we had to be cautious. However, as we ate up our food supplies, that weight could be replaced with dinosaur bones.

In the morning Dan and Buddy were anxious to get started fossil hunting. They hiked to the south end of the island to see if they could find any bone material on the bluff. There was an interesting seam in the strata that looked like it might hold some promise of fossils. They worked all morning and found just a few small scraps. After lunch, George, Mike, and John went to help them. Everyone then hiked over to the Liscomb Bone Bed via the top of the bluff on the tundra. We wanted to do more collecting and to shoot some video of the bone bed. It was about a three-mile walk. When we reached the top of the bluff, the landscape was flat and dotted with hundreds of lakes. Some were no larger than a small pond and others covered several acres.

On the way we came across a playful red fox. He was very interested in us. Maybe this was the first time he had ever seen a human. He didn't seem to mind us at all and followed us along, jumping through the tundra much like a family dog would have done. He came as close as 50 feet to Mike. As we neared the place where we needed to hike down the bluff to the bone bed, we decided to have a short siesta on the tundra. It had turned into a beautiful sunny day with a slight breeze. The tundra grasses were plentiful and the shrubs were short and scattered, so it didn't take long to find a soft spot for a nap. It was hard to believe the Arctic Ocean was about 20 miles due north and the temperature was in the high sixties (F). It was a very pleasant time. Most of us didn't even seem to mind the mosquitoes for a while. They were especially thick, due to the calm wind and warm air. Clouds of mosquitoes swarmed around us and some crawled over us looking for any exposed skin. Our thoughts went back to Umiat and the start of our journey. We joked with each other about when we got off the bush plane and made our mad scramble to get our headnets and find our bug dope. Then O.J. Smith's words came back to us, "Oh, you get used to the bugs after a while." Well, I guess we finally had.

The view of the Colville River Valley from the top of the bluff was spectacular. Although we were only 150 feet above the river, we probably could see for ten miles or so to the south and east. To the north and west, all that we could see was a flat, grassy tundra. The tundra looked flatter than it actually is. While walking across it we found many small cracks and gullies several feet wide, which acted as drainage ditches. Some were deep and camouflaged by willows and other shrubs growing in them. Most of us stumbled into the hidden cracks at least once. It hadn't rained up here for a while because the high tundra was dry and dusty beneath the shrubs and grasses. The low tundra, closer to the river, was a bit more soggy because of the poor drainage it had. Occasionally the tundra had a hill on it that might be described more like a mound. They were 25 to 100 feet in diameter and 10 to 30 feet high. Most of these features were "pingos" which were the result of frost heaving in the tundra soils. As water freezes and expands in the tundra soils, it sometimes forces the soil upward, forming these small hills.

After our nap, we found a gully and hiked down it to the bottom of the bluff. Dan had a hard time. After watching the video we had shot that day, we counted that he fell five times walking down the gully. He was still pretty exhausted from his quicksand experience. We collected a few more bone samples, and George shot some video of our activities. We walked back to camp along the base of the bluff. It was more difficult walking here than along the top of the bluff, but it was about one mile shorter. This walk probably would have been impossible if the river had been any higher. One

AFTER OUR AFTERNOON "SIESTA" ON THE TUN-
DRA, WE PREPARED TO HIKE DOWN THE BLUFF
TO COLLECT SOME MORE BONES. GEORGE SHOT
THE VIDEO AND TOOK MANY OF THE PICTURES
DURING THE TRIP. NOTE THAT HE IS THE ONLY
ONE WEARING A HEADNET. FROM LEFT TO
RIGHT: GEORGE, JOHN, BUDDY, AND MIKE

can get from the base of the bluff to the island by choosing
their steps carefully as they cross the high water stream channel. The channel was full of sticks, brush, and mud, and

many tall willows grew there which were difficult to wade through. We crossed one area of deep mud. John walked quickly, sinking just past his ankles. If he had stopped, he may have ended up like Dan did two days earlier. It looked as if this channel had only been dried up for a few days. When the river was higher, last week, water was probably flowing through here.

We were all pretty tired after our hike back to camp, and some even had blisters on their feet. It was no wonder since we had damp feet and had been wearing hip boots for the past week. After eating our evening meal, some of us went to the river to wash up. As we were standing in the river washing, we had a swarm of mosquitoes around us. Every time the breeze picked up, the mosquitoes would have to beat their wings a little faster to stay around us. The pitch of their wings beating would get higher and lower depending on the breeze. It sounded like a miniature symphony.

We washed all the DEET (N-Diethyl-m-tolumide) off our hands, arms, and head. It felt good to get the chemicals off, though the water is extremely cold. DEET is powerful stuff. It dries out and cracks your skin. All of us were suffering from deep splits in the corner of our fingers that refused to heal. We constantly would have to apply hand lotion. When our faces would sweat, the DEET would get in our eyes and they would sting and burn. When it got on our lips, they would burn and then go numb. We also found out earlier on our trip that it melted plastic. After applying it to our hands it melted the plastic boat paddles, causing our hands to stick to them. When handling our camera while taking pictures, we had to carefully remove all the DEET from our hands or else it would melt the camera. George and Mike had an especially rough time because George was constantly documenting the trip with video and photographs and Mike was using the G.P.S. They had to go without DEET protection on their hands or else wear gloves to be able to handle the plastic equipment. Buddy had a bottle of DEET break open in his pocket and it soaked his brand new Swiss Army knife that his wife had bought him for the trip. Buddy was really proud of that knife but after its encounter with the DEET, it was so melted that it looked like he had thrown it into a campfire!

It was a challenge to go to the bathroom with all the mosquitoes. One had to try to wait for a windy part of the day, or else when you dropped your pants you would instantly have a hundred skeeters biting your backside. You quickly lost the urge to go. We were wondering how Dan could use his folding toilet seat, since it sat way up in the air. He said he would apply the DEET to his rear end before going. But once, he must have put too much on. . . . The seat was plastic, so you can imagine what happened. He melted and molded the seat right to . . . you get the picture! We suggested that next time we come up here, he should make a mosquito net skirt for his seat, so he wouldn't have that problem again!

We all got in our tents about 9:30, and started making preparations for the final push to Nuiqsut in the morning. If we paddled hard and the wind was in the right direction it might be possible to make it in one day. Our bags were quite a bit lighter and roomier because of all the food we had eaten.

We started with 28 MRE meals. On some days we ate really well, and on others we would never get the chance to eat until the end of the day. So we didn't really know how many days' rations we had left. Some of us were down to four meals. The MRE's were surprisingly good. In each MRE are two large crackers. The crackers are very dry, and you get either cheese, jelly, or peanut butter to put on them. Of the three, the cheese spread is the best and peanut butter is the worst. Swallowing the very dry crackers is just too hard with the sticky peanut butter. It usually sticks to the roof of your mouth. John had an unusual streak of cheese — and everyone was envious. It seemed as though when everybody checked to see what John got, he had cheese and they had peanut butter. They jokingly accused him of stealing their cheese and replacing it with his peanut butter at night when everyone else was asleep.

We could hear much activity coming from each man's tent as they packed and secured their gear. Getting back in the "river mode" was hard after being camped for three days. John and Mike had met earlier in the day and spent a couple hours poring over the maps and entering checkpoints into the G.P.S. Tomorrow we would really have to keep our heads up, because as the Colville River approaches the Arctic Ocean it splits into hundreds of different channels and only one led to the village of Nuiqsut. A large portion of each day was spent maintaining our bodies and equipment. Despite how tired one was at the end of the day, there were always notes to take, cameras and guns to clean, and mosquitoes to kill in your tent before you laid down to sleep. Usually, George could be heard softly singing praises as we drifted off to sleep.

THE WAVES AT OCEAN POINT ALMOST
SANK OUR SMALL RUBBER RAFTS.

10

Stranded, Rescued, Jailed!

Wednesday, July 20

Our alarm clocks (mosquitoes) jarred us awake at 5:00 a.m.! The day promised to be a big one! During the night it drizzled a few times, and light rain was falling as we woke up. The wind had shifted and was coming from the south! We knew we had a south wind because the mosquitoes were hovering on the lee side (north side) of our tents trying to get out of the wind. Buddy, Dan, and Mike had eaten a cold meal in their tents for breakfast. While they were waiting for the others they carried gear down to the beach and loaded the rafts. By the time everyone was ready to leave at 7:15, the wind had picked up in speed. John felt we needed to tie all the rafts together again. However, Mike convinced him that we should try it in our separate rafts for a while and see if we could make better time.

The south wind was great. Between the current and the wind we made seven or eight miles in just two hours! However, by the time we reached Ocean Point, the wind had increased and began to blow us into the beach. They must call this area "Ocean Point" because of the waves there. These were the biggest we saw on the Colville. They were about two feet high and often broke against our small rafts, soaking us with water. It seemed like we were rafting on the ocean!

It was a fight and a struggle to get around Ocean Point. We finally made it, only to be stranded on the beach. We used the time while we were stranded to eat a cold snack and then started off again. We continued to have a tough time against the wind and waves. The river was getting wider, the wind was getting stronger, the waves were getting higher, and the temperature was getting colder. We paddled through several giant dust storms making it difficult to see. A cold front began to move in on us, and it began to drizzle and get foggy. Our boats had to be walked along the shore most of the time. Making any gains down the river by paddling was impossible, and even by pulling the boats we made little progress. We began to doubt. We wouldn't make it to Nuiqsut today. If the weather continued like this, we might not make it before our pickup time Friday afternoon.

By 3:00 we beached and waited for a break in the wind. The wind had shifted to the west, and was blowing us into the eastern side of the river. This concerned us, because we needed to be on the western side of the river to get the correct tributary channel for Nuiqsut. We had something to eat and waited four hours for the wind to die down. During this time we observed a large cloud bank roll in from the southwest — the weather was deteriorating rapidly. We didn't take the temperature, but it must have been close to 40 degrees (F) and falling. It was especially cold considering what the wind chill factor must have been. Most of us had on every bit of clothing we could muster, which included two layers of wool clothing over our long underwear, wind breaker, rain suit, and life jacket. We were still cold, but we didn't have anything else we could wear. We were also worried about how wet our gear was getting. The boats had taken on quite a bit of water because of the large waves. Our duffels were soaked on the outside and lying in several inches of water in the bottoms of our boats. We now had to bail water out of the rafts, besides paddling and pulling. We hoped we had wrapped our sleeping bags and clothes in enough garbage bags so they wouldn't get wet. Only time would tell. It looked like it was going to be a miserable night for camping.

We hunkered down on the beach and tried to keep as warm as possible. By 7:00 p.m. the storm hadn't let up. John and Dan said we should try to push ahead. The others thought that it was just too dangerous and we should set up camp and wait it out. Maybe we could push on when the storm broke even if it were during the middle of the night. John convinced everyone that the only way to stay warm was to get back into the rafts and paddle. We tied all three of the rafts together like a train and removed some gear from the lead raft and placed it into the other two rafts making room for the five of us. All of us paddling together was like a bigger motor. All of our strength united might make it possible to continue on the river and get to the other side. The five of us got in the lead raft and began to paddle with all of our might against the wind and waves. It seemed like a never-ending nightmare. We kept paddling until we couldn't paddle anymore. Every time one of us wanted to give up, we would look at the others and see them still paddling. After paddling 45 minutes, we looked back and saw we were still only 100 feet from shore. The wind and waves were just too strong. Our hearts sank with despair. We continued our valiant struggle, and finally made it across the river to the western shore. We were forced to get out and pull the rafts again, but it was easier than paddling. By 9:30 p.m. all of us were wet, tired, shivering with cold, and hungry. We were totally exhausted and could go no further. We had only covered 17 of the 35 miles toward Nuiqsut. We began to worry. If we had weather this bad for the next two days, we would not make it to our pickup point by Friday afternoon. We were experiencing the lowest point during the trip, all of us in danger of hypothermia. We could do nothing else but stop and start to set up camp.

We were in a bad situation. We were stranded on an exposed beach, surrounded by quicksand. The nearest solid ground was 300 feet away from us. The quicksand would have to be crossed to get there. George volunteered to be the first one to attempt it. The rest of us sat on the edge of our

STRANDED ON THE BEACH WAITING FOR THE WIND TO
DIE DOWN AND THE STORM TO PASS.

rafts to keep from sinking as we watched. George didn't make it very far. The wet sand shook and quivered like Jello and an area the size of a car sagged and filled with water behind him as he walked. As he turned and made his way back to the rafts, he had to avoid the area he had just walked across because it was now too soft to support him. The quicksand would barely support one man moving quickly — if he didn't stop. There was no way it would support the five of us and the many trips back and forth carrying our heavy duffel bags. Staying in the rafts on the beach was out of the question. The waves breaking against the sides of the raft were throwing spray into the air and getting everything wet.

The decision to push on earlier in the day instead of setting up camp to wait out the storm was weighing heavily on everyone's mind. When we had stopped paddling and got out of the rafts, we became extremely cold. The early stages of hypothermia were starting. We had been out on the river for 14 hours with only one meal. Things were looking very grim.

John's side note: Looking back over our circumstances, I have to say as a group leader, that the team certainly impressed me. Although our morale was at an all-time low, I never heard a single word of complaint. I was blessed as a leader. I couldn't have been with a better group of men. Somehow we knew the Lord was with us and He would provide in our difficult circumstances. "For he shall give his angels charge over thee, to keep thee in all thy ways. They shall bear thee up in [their] hands, lest thou dash thy foot against a stone" (Ps. 91:11-12;KJV). "Not that I speak in respect of want: for I have learned, in whatsoever state I am, [therewith] to be content. I know both how to be abased, and I know how to abound: every where and in all things I am instructed both to be full and to be hungry, both to abound and to suffer need. I can do all things through Christ which strengtheneth me" (Phil. 4:11-13;KJV). We tried to keep a positive attitude, but it was hard.

Then it happened — Mike, delirious with cold, was shouting and waving his arms around. Buddy must have been delirious too, because he started shouting and waving! It wasn't until then that the rest of the team saw what Mike and Buddy were waving at! There were two motor boats full of Eskimos, heading downriver toward Nuiqsut! They had been hunting and fishing upriver and were the same boats we had seen several days earlier. Mike was the first one to hear them above the sound of the wind and rain. When he turned to look, the first boat had already gone past. It was with desperation that he started to holler and wave at the second boat while frantically digging in his shirt pocket for the aerial signal flares. He had carried the flares for just such an emergency.

Mike and Buddy finally succeeded in getting the attention of the last boat and it slowed and turned toward shore. The next problem was how to communicate with these Eskimos. We had been warned beforehand to avoid the Eskimos at Nuiqsut, and we weren't even sure if they spoke English. Mike waded out in the river as far as he could as the Eskimo boat neared. They got as close as they could without getting hung up on the sand bar. We were relieved to find out that they did speak English. Mike yelled back and forth between the boat and shore, negotiating a deal. Yes, the Eskimos would be glad to tow us into Nuiqsut for $50.00! It was the best money we ever spent! It was almost as if they were angels sent from God!

The ride to Nuiqsut was long and cold. None of us remember shivering with cold more than during that ride. We had tied our three rafts together again for the tow to Nuiqsut. George took the opportunity while he had it to eat two MRE meals. That shows just how depleted our bodies were because each MRE supplied 2,500 calories.

During the tow we had an opportunity to study our rescuers. There were four Eskimos in the boat — two teenage boys and their girlfriends. The two girls were dressed in traditional Eskimo fur-lined parkas. The boys wore what any teenager back home might wear, blue jeans and a hooded sweatshirt. The river was nothing but a series of wide-sweeping S curves, where the wind would have swept our

RESCUED BY ESKIMO TEENAGERS. MIKE IS SHIVERING
FROM THE COLD BOAT RIDE.

rafts mercilessly against one bank after another. As the hours
and miles fell behind us, Buddy would say repeatedly, "We
would never have made it!" He was right.

We were within five miles of Nuiqsut when our lead
raft began to take on water. George and John had had trouble
with it all week, but it was only a slow leak. Now it was
massive. There were several inches of water in the bottom
of the boat. The Eskimos wanted to know if we wanted to
stop — no way! Dan discovered the hole in the bottom where
the water was spurting in like a drinking fountain. Apparently a patch had come loose. The pressure of the water

caused by the speed of the tow probably caused the already weak patch to fail. Buddy, Dan, and Mike could not bail the water out fast enough. George and John could only watch helplessly from their positions in the second and third rafts. After they discovered the hole, Dan stood on it the rest of the way to Nuiqsut, as a temporary patch. The other guys occasionally bailed with one of the tin mess kit bowls we had. It worked! There was no way we were going to stop!

After a two-hour ride we saw our first glimpse of real civilization since we left Umiat. It had been a long, cold ride but it was worth it. We arrived in Nuiqsut at 11:30 p.m. We gave the driver of our boat, Jimmy Oyagak, $80 instead of $50. The ride was well worth it. We would never have made it otherwise. To be taken from the wilderness of Alaska and thrown into the Eskimo village of Nuiqsut was quite a culture shock. Here it was 11:30 at night, and half the village had turned out to see the spectacle of five sorry-looking white men being rescued and towed. The village has no telephone system so they use CB radios in their homes and boats. Jimmy had radioed ahead to tell everyone that he was towing in five "tunics" (white men), and quite a crowd turned out to see us.

There was a grassy area near the boat ramp where we began to set up camp. The peace officer of the village came down to see what we were doing. He introduced himself (Tom Thomas) and said they were about ready to come looking for us. Apparently O.J. had gotten his days mixed up and thought we were going to be in Nuiqsut several days ago. They became worried that something had happened to us and were going to come looking for us in the morning. Tom soon left. We wanted to get our tents up as soon as possible. We were exhausted.

Our duffel bags were extremely heavy because they were waterlogged. When we lifted them, the water poured out. It would be a cold miserable night, but somehow we felt better knowing we were in civilization again. As we were unpacking our soggy tents and sleeping bags, Tom came

MIKE AND BUDDY JAILED AT NUIQSUT. HAVE YOU EVER SEEN TWO GUYS HAPPIER TO BE IN JAIL?

back and asked if we would like to stay in a garage for the night. (Apparently he had left to see if it would be okay with his superior officer, Jack McFarland.) Would we like to stay in a garage for the night? Of course! A garage would seem like a room at the Waldorf-Astoria!

He had a big double cab, four-wheel-drive pickup. We quickly loaded all of our stuff into the back for the short ride to the police station. When we got there, he said we had a choice — we could spend the night in the garage or in the jail cells. Of course we chose the jail cells! Buddy said he never thought he would be glad to go to jail, but this jail sentence came from heaven. What an end to an amazing day. Who would have ever thought just three hours ago, while setting up our tents on wet, cold sand, that we would be spending the night in a warm, dry, mosquito-free jail? The Lord sure does have a sense of humor! What an amazing provider He is! When we were at our lowest point, the Lord marvelously provided for us.

In the warmth of the jail cell, we could smell ourselves for the first time. Five unwashed bodies and all that wet wool clothing made quite a stench! Yet we were too tired to care as we dropped into the exhausted sleep of dead men in our warm, dry home.

THE TEAM IN FRONT OF THE NUIQSUT PUBLIC SAFETY
BUILDING (THE "JAIL"). FROM LEFT TO RIGHT:
TOM, MIKE, JOHN, BUDDY, DAN, AND GEORGE.

11

Life in an Eskimo Village

Thursday, July 21
    We all slept in. The earliest any of us even moved was
9:30 or so. We could not use the shower, but there was a

sink and flush toilet. What a luxury! About 11:30 a.m. some of us went to the community center to use the satellite phone. John wanted to call Umiat and tell O.J. to come and pick up his rafts, and all of us wanted to call home. We had a good laugh telling our spouses and families that we were in jail!

One of the officers took us to the coin laundry. They also happened to have a coin shower — praise the Lord! It was one of the best showers we ever had. We all thought we had gotten a good suntan, but it was gone after two minutes in the shower. While waiting for his wool clothes to dry (they took forever), John threw one of his MRE's in the dryer to warm it up. It worked! All of our duffels, clothes, and tents were muddy from the day before. We really made a mess of things at the jail and laundry. This happens to be the only laundromat on the North Slope of Alaska. People fly here from Barrow and Prudoe Bay just to wash their clothes! That would be a 100-mile plane ride for the sole purpose of washing clothes. They told us some people bring five or six large garbage bags full of dirty laundry with them. Wouldn't you hate to be on that plane! While at the laundry we met Jimmy again (he was the one who had towed us). He agreed to take us in his boat out into the Arctic Ocean. Our adventure would continue!

After doing our laundry and taking that long-awaited shower, we went back to the police station for lunch. Dan fired up his methanol stove in the middle of the garage and we ate. Being able to eat in a relatively mosquito-free environment without mosquito headnets was wonderful. We did the same for dinner a few hours later. Following dinner we had to haul our muddy rafts up to the gravel landing strip a quarter-mile away for O.J. to pick up. We hauled one boat up and then an Eskimo offered to put the other two rafts in the back of his truck and take them to the airport for us. We obliged. The airport is the lifeline of this community. A dozen or more airplanes land here daily, connecting Nuiqsut with the outside world.

The natives of Nuiqsut were very friendly and helpful. The town has about 350 Eskimos, and the only white people in the town are the two peace officers and their wives. All of the buildings are on stilts. Building in areas of permafrost is difficult because the upper two feet of frost thaws during the summer, making the surface a muddy, sloppy mess. To counteract this, they drill deep holes and sink the posts into permafrost, using it for a foundation. Most of the houses are small, maybe 24 x 40 feet, with two bedrooms. Most of them cost $150,000 or more to build because of the high cost of delivering building materials here. However, the Alaskan natives have more money than their southern counterparts in the lower 48 states. Each native gets a sizable sum from the federal and state governments each year from revenues produced from the oil industry on the North Slope. This explained all the new cars and boats we saw in this odd little village.

The town of Nuiqsut was founded in the mid-1970s. Outcasts from Barrow and other Eskimo towns founded the village on the North Slope. According to the officers, this town has more crimes per capita than any other on the Slope. Supposedly, this town is full of ax murderers, rapists, thieves, and other criminals. This surprised us because we had encountered nothing but friendly people here. The kids were especially curious. They would ask us hundreds of questions. "Why are you here?" "Why are you in jail?" "What is that you are eating?" They would touch and pluck at our clothing and gear and ask, "Can I have this?" We wondered

if this were the reason the police officers offered us the jail for lodging. There were no motels or restaurants in Nuiqsut.

The officers get about ten calls a day — usually nothing serious. Sometimes they have to break up a domestic quarrel or shoot a rabid dog or fox. We learned that most of the foxes up here have rabies and are extremely dangerous. This gave us another reason to praise the Lord that we didn't have an incident with the red fox three days ago on the tundra. As we sat and talked with the officers that evening, it seemed like they were lonely and enjoyed talking with us. It isn't often they get to "civilization." Tom was an avid outdoorsman (one almost has to be to live up here) and told us many stories of his hunting trips. One story was about a guy who got stuck in quicksand up to his waist and couldn't get out. A grizzly bear came along and killed him, taking him apart piece by piece with his huge claws!

The townspeople seem quite bored. There is not much to do here, and many of them just drive around town in their vehicles. Occasionally someone would be pulling their new boat through the one-square-mile town to show it off.

We were surprised to see so many cars and trucks because there are no roads leading to Nuiqsut. They even have a town bus that makes 15-minute circuits on the town's gravel roads. We found out they transport most of their large belongings in the winter. The Colville River freezes solid and becomes a road on which vehicles as large as semi trucks can travel. Many of them will drive their snowmobile or truck to Prudoe Bay (the nearest town) during the winter freeze. The peace officers told us that some go there to get liquor. Surprisingly, there were no bars or liquor stores in Nuiqsut. Drinking here is illegal. Their crime rate would be even higher if they allowed it. Many of them watch lots of TV. There are dozens of large satellite dishes pointing south toward the horizon.

As the day came to a close, we found ourselves back at the jail, visiting with Tom and Jack. We were hoping they would invite us to spend another night in their comfortable cells. We were getting very tired and anxious, when Dan boldly asked, "May we spend the night?" When they graciously granted us permission, we were happy to be "inmates" once again!

THE ARCTIC OCEAN. FROM LEFT TO RIGHT:
JOHN, BUDDY, MIKE, AND GEORGE.

12

Stranded in the Arctic Ocean on a Caribou Hunt!

Friday, July 22

We got up at 6:00 a.m. and put on our warmest clothes and rain gear. It was 40 degrees (F) with a light mist falling.

We talked Jimmy into taking us the ten miles down river to the Arctic Ocean. He had a 19-foot fiberglass boat shell with a 75 horse outboard on the back. We paid him $50 for the ride. (Dan decided not to go — he stayed behind to work on a dentistry article. Personally, we think he had experienced enough adventure for a while.) On the way down the Colville, we discovered that the river split into many distributaries (channels — the opposite of tributaries) and became shallow as we came to the end of the river and progressed onto the river delta.

At one point on the river the mosquitoes were really bad and Mike looked at Jimmy and thought to himself, *He doesn't have any biting him, I wonder if he has some secret Eskimo lotion?* About that time, Jimmy reached in his pocket and pulled out a bottle of OFF bug spray and asked, "You guys got this stuff on?" Here he had been wondering the same thing, *Do the white guys have some magic lotion for the bugs?*

The Eskimos said that 40,000 caribou had gathered close to the ocean for the short summer. We saw two small herds of 400 to 1,000 animals. The caribou were about ready to migrate south over the Brooks Range for the winter. One herd was on a small island in the river completely lacking plants. All the animals stay together in a single herd — the bulls, cows, and calves. Seeing so many of these wild animals together in one place was exhilarating. We wondered why they were in a place with no plants. Maybe to get away from the bugs? They told us each animal loses up to a quart of blood a week from the mosquitoes. That's a lot of mosquito bites! When the caribou became tormented by the swarms of flies, bees, and mosquitoes, they would break into a run to try to get away from their pests. Life is hard for them. Sin has effected not only people but animals and plants as well. The whole earth groans. "For we know that the whole creation groaneth and travaileth in pain together until now" (Rom. 8:22;KJV). Won't it be wonderful when Christ rules and there will be no more suffering? (See Isa. 65 and Rev. 21.)

After a half-hour boat ride, we could see the open ocean ahead of us. Along the horizon we could see the white polar ice cap. Jimmy took us about 12 miles out so we could get a good view of it. He didn't want to get too close because the chunks of ice in the ocean became more numerous as we approached the cap. In fact, we had a bumpy ride as we hit some chunks and ran over others. Jimmy stopped the boat and we sat awhile gazing at the ice pack. It was about this time that Mike looked over at Buddy and asked, "Where is your life jacket?" Buddy shot back, "Where is yours?" After feeling how cold the water was, both decided it didn't matter. One wouldn't last long in the water if the boat sank. The water was cold, but was not as salty as other ocean water — probably because of the large volume of fresh water being introduced by the Colville River. The ocean was not as choppy as we had expected. The water was rougher on the Colville River two days ago! We saw no wildlife in the ocean. The polar bears usually summer out on the cap and then come inland for the winter. They are rarely seen.

We saw snow squalls out on the ice pack, and we were in awe knowing that we were this close to the top of the world. After shooting some pictures, we dipped our feet in the Arctic Ocean. Talk about cold! We were literally in an ocean of ice water! Our hearts skipped a beat when the motor didn't catch the first time and we joked about having to paddle back to shore.

On our way back, Jimmy tried to find the same delta channel we had left one hour before. The only problem was the tide had gone out, and we had trouble getting back into the main river channel. Suddenly, Jimmy shut the engine down. The prop was churning up the mud because the water was only two feet deep. The first thing we did was to look at our watches. We were grounded a mile out in the Arctic Ocean on the Colville River delta and we had a plane to catch in four hours. We jumped out of the boat to find deeper water. This wasn't anything new to us. We had done this drill often in the week before. Still, who would have guessed we'd be wading around, a mile out in the Arctic Ocean! The ocean water was very dark in color and one could only see about a foot deep. We probed with the boat paddles ahead of us as we pushed the boat and waded in the thigh-deep water. We didn't want anyone accidentally falling into a drop-off. Much to our relief, we were unstuck in about 15 minutes. How much more adventure could we take? Thanks, Lord, for providing again.

Actually it shouldn't have surprised us that the water was so shallow a mile out in the ocean. Rivers carry an incredible amount of mud and sediment into the oceans. The Mississippi River carries two million tons of mud into the Gulf of Mexico every day! The Colville isn't quite that large, but it still carries a lot of mud into the ocean, making it very shallow. Currently the Mississippi River delta is about 250 miles in length, much of it being under water. Because of the large volume of sediment being introduced, it is growing in length one mile every 16 years! Assuming current rates of sedimentation, this makes the delta about 4,000 years old — much younger than evolutionary estimates!

We saw a large caribou herd on our way back up the

river to Nuiqsut. Jimmy had met two of his cousins in another boat and they decided to go into the herd and shoot a bull to take back with them. Hunting caribou is not anything like hunting deer in Ohio, where we have to be quiet and wait for the prey to come to us. The Eskimos walked nonchalantly into the middle of the panicking herd. We had to wonder why the Eskimos didn't hunt from their boats. Their high-powered rifles and scopes should have made it easy to pick out a bull from a far distance. The caribou began to panic and stampede. The Eskimos stood in the middle of the herd. It is a wonder that they didn't get trampled. All we could see was antlers and dust from where we were in the boat. Mike could not hold himself back. Jumping out of the boat he sprinted to the vicinity of the Eskimos. Finally we heard several shots.

One young Eskimo had just downed his first bull caribou. It was a fine trophy. We didn't expect to be part of an Eskimo caribou hunt! What a thrill! We helped them field dress the bull and carry the meat to the boat. The Eskimos use the entire animal, and we mean *all*. An Eskimo custom is to take a bite out of the raw kidney of the animal. After Jimmy took a huge bite, Buddy and Mike decided to try it. George and John declined. John refused, because he knew what the function of the kidney is, and based on its function, its probable taste. Buddy confirmed his expectations after spitting out his small bite. He held it in his mouth only long enough for a picture.

Along with the meat, they kept the hide and head. The dead caribou showed us a close-up look of its hard Arctic life. Small biting flies and mosquitoes blanketed the animal's face and body. They were in the caribou's eyes, nose, ears, and genitals. Even the death of this animal didn't release it from its insect predators. They continued to swarm the carcass looking for the still-cooling blood. Someone said shooting the caribou ended its misery. After we packed the meat back to the boat we were surprised to see some of the caribou herd returning to the area.

The Eskimos are allowed to kill up to five caribou a day. The caribou are only in their area for a short time, so they have to take advantage of them when they can. The Eskimos have several ice houses in which they store the meat. They dig holes deep into the permafrost where the meat keeps nicely. The other main staple of their diet is "muktuk," and is considered a delicacy. This is the hide of the whale with a layer of blubber below. It is dried until it is

JIMMY WITH HIS TWO COUSINS, SHOWING OFF THEIR CARIBOU TROPHY.

JIMMY EATING THE RAW CARIBOU KIDNEY.

crisp and crunchy. Last year they killed three whales that fed their entire village for the year.

We thought we were finished with all of our adventures, but on our way back to Nuiqsut part of the herd was crossing the river. We pulled right up to some animals swimming in the water. There were dozens of them swimming all around us. We could reach out and touch them. What an experience! How great the Lord has been to us in allowing

CARIBOU CROSSING THE COLVILLE RIVER.

us to experience everything we have. It has been one surprise after another.

We made it back to Nuiqsut about 2:00, expecting our
pickup plane to arrive at 4:00. We ate the last of our MRE's
in the garage jail. We had planned our rations well! The peace
officers let us load our gear in the back of their truck for the
short trip over to the landing strip and then we waited anx-
iously. At the sound of every plane we looked outside to see
if it was ours. Finally, it arrived about 5:30, over an hour
late. We left Nuiqsut at 5:45 p.m. on our bush plane flight
back to Fairbanks. The plane was so heavily loaded that we
used up most of the gravel airstrip to get airborne. However,
before leaving the North Slope we talked the pilot into one
last glimpse of the Arctic Ocean. The view of the delta, ocean,

and the winding river on which we had struggled so much was unforgettable. We could see icebergs floating in the ocean. The village of Nuiqsut looked like a postage stamp from the air. As we viewed the winding river below, we had a flood of memories. Everything that we had gone through to collect a few dinosaur bones seemed unreal now. The bones must have something special in them. Tears came to our eyes as we were reminded of the awesome God we serve.

It was cloudy for most of the trip back to Fairbanks. Most of the guys took the opportunity for a well-deserved nap. When we got to Fairbanks, it was a mad scramble at the airport. We had to unpack our gear and sort out what belonged to whom. Additionally, we had to find the gear we

THE COLVILLE RIVER FLOWING INTO THE ARCTIC OCEAN. THIS PICTURE SHOWS THE MANY DISTRIBUTARIES OF THE COLVILLE RIVER DELTA.

A CARIBOU HERD CROSSING THE COLVILLE RIVER ON
THE NORTH SLOPE OF ALASKA.

had left behind in the hangar for storage. We re-packed all of it and distributed the dinosaur bones among us. About one mile from the airport we had a good hot hamburger and fries on an outside deck at a restaurant. It tasted so good to eat something besides an MRE. We weren't able to get Dan's Dairy Queen Blizzard. He had been craving one for over a week. The Fairbanks Dairy Queen burned down several years ago and had never been rebuilt. As we ate and shared our memories, we thanked the Lord for the good times, the bad times, and the deeper trust we had gained in Him. We also thanked the Lord for the mosquito-free outdoors in which we were eating! We overheard several tourists talking about how bad the mosquitoes were in Fairbanks, but compared with where we had just come from, we didn't even notice any. All of us started laughing when we heard them say that the next stop on their tour was Barrow, Alaska. We all thought to ourselves, *They'll be sorry!*

We left Fairbanks for Anchorage and home close to midnight. It was a great feeling to be on a commercial airliner leaving Alaska with so many memories. We got to see the sun set in the west as we taxied out onto the runway. It was the first time it had gotten dark since we left Fairbanks 11 days ago at the start of our journey. It was a strange feeling. Once we were airborne and higher up, we saw the sun set again behind the mighty Denali (Mt. McKinley).

Saturday, July 23

George, Buddy, and John returned home via Anchorage, Seattle, Denver, and Indianapolis. Dan flew with us to Seattle and then he went on to Chicago and Columbus. We left Mike in Fairbanks. He spent an extra week touring some mountains in southern Alaska. It was an experience trying to get the 80-pound jawbone through the airport. John decided to carry it on the plane with him. He wasn't going to trust it to the baggage handlers! It was wrapped in a plastic tarp and then duct-taped. John put it inside his backpack. Of course every time we went through the x-ray machines the operator had to know what was inside. John had to completely unwrap the muddy package in Denver. It was great to finally get to Indianapolis. What an adventure!

All of the team members were experienced outdoorsmen. Most of us have had experience in fossil hunting. We've had many grand adventures before this trip. However, this expedition will always rank as one of our most memorable. We will use it to witness for our mighty God for years. What started out to be a dinosaur hunt turned into the adventure of a lifetime. We could clearly see God's hand in all of our life-threatening situations and discoveries. He is certainly a God of action. Whoever thinks the Christian life is boring is seriously mistaken!

As we reminisced and wrote the story of our trip, we were humbled. All of us grew closer to our Creator because of the experience. What an awesome God we serve. God works through people, and we only need to be available. Praises be to our Creator and Lord who made all of this possible and sustained us through the wilds of the Colville River on the Alaskan tundra.

"Thou art worthy, O Lord, to receive glory and honour and power: for thou hast created all things, and for thy pleasure they are and were created" (Rev. 4:11). "And I saw another angel fly in the midst of heaven, having the everlasting gospel to preach unto them that dwell on the earth, and to every nation, and kindred, and tongue, and people, Saying with a loud voice, Fear God, and give glory to him; for the hour of his judgment is come: and worship him that made heaven, and earth, and the sea, and the fountains of waters" (Rev. 14:6-7).

13

Where Do We Go from Here?
A Postscript

There is still much work and research that needs to be done with the bones that we found in Alaska. One project being completed is a total chemical analysis of the bones. We will be looking for any original biomolecules that might remain in them. Another is the description and publication of the large mandible that we discovered. The bones have also raised questions among creationists as to their depositional history. Did the dinosaurs that left these deposits die during Noah's flood, or is it possible they may have lived after the flood? How did some bones become petrified while others have very little mineral content in them at all? When did the bones become frozen and how long have they been that way? These and other problems will need to be addressed in the future.

Scientific research is healthy as it helps us search for answers as we seek to defend our faith (1 Pet. 3:15). If we can find numerous biomolecules in the Alaskan bones, it may help us to show that these bones can't realistically be 70 million years old. For instance, scientists from the University of Montana were surprised to find what might be the chemical remains of blood cells in the bones of a *Tyrannosaurus rex*. Even the scientists admit the cells should have long ago disintegrated. The process of biochemical decay starts soon after death. Imagining how these molecules could stay preserved for millions and millions of years is difficult.

The type of analysis that we are doing with these bones is time consuming and expensive. If you would like more information on how you could contribute to the process financially, contact the Creation Research — Science Education Foundation (CRSEF), P.O. Box 292, Columbus, OH 43216. A board member of CRSEF may be contacted at (614) 837-3097. A 30-minute video about the trip can be purchased from CRSEF for $15, which will help with the cost of this project.

Many times we have been asked how to pursue a career in creation-related subjects or just how to get involved. There are a number of ways and fields you could pursue. We have listed some resources that you might desire to check out. You might also consider becoming an active part of a local or national creation ministry. Make yourself known and be available. Seek God's guidance.

To learn more about creation and to find information that will help you defend your faith, contact:

Answers in Genesis
P.O. Box 6330
Florence, KY 41022

Institute for Creation Research
P.O. Box 2667
El Cajon, CA 92021

CRSEF
P.O. Box 292
Columbus, OH 43216

Creation Science Foundation
P.O. Box 6302
Acacia Ridge DC, QLD 4110
Australia

Cedarville College in Cedarville, Ohio, believes and teaches a literal interpretation of Genesis. If you are interested in an education in the sciences or other fields, contact its admissions department at 1-800-CEDARVILLE or write Cedarville College, P.O. Box 601, Cedarville, OH 45314.

Questions to Discuss

1. Why did God let the five men struggle with the elements such as quicksand when the expedition was bathed in prayer? (Romans 8:20-23, Genesis 3, Job 23:10)

2. Do you think the men would have still gone on this expedition had they known the dangers? (Acts 6:41, Philippians 1:29, Acts 20:24, 1 Peter 4:12-13, 1 Samuel 17:45-47)

3. Why did the men have to work so hard to find the bones? (Ephesians 6:11, 1 Peter 5:8, James 4:7)

4. Why did the men have to paddle a raft instead of using a motor boat or flying to the spot? (1 Peter 5:7, Psalms 55:22, Psalms 34:19)

5. What lessons did the men learn? (Psalms 4:5, Genesis 6:17, Romans 1:20, Romans 5:12-14)

6. Do you think that teamwork was an important part of the expedition? (1 Corinthians 12:25, Romans 5:3-5, Genesis 2:18, John 13:14-17)

7. If the evidence indicates the dinosaur bones aren't old, will the world listen? (2 Peter 3:3-6, Romans 1:18-22, Proverbs 1:7, 1 Corinthians 2:14)

8. Do you think more research should be done in this area? (1 Peter 3:15, 2 Timothy 2:15)

9. Do you think the explorers responded as Christians should?

(Matthew 5:16, 2 Corinthians 5:20)

10. How can you use the explorers' discoveries to defend your faith?

(1 Peter 3:15, Genesis 1:24-25, Genesis 6:17)

We are all descendents of the first man, Adam, who rebelled against God and brought sin and death into the world. We, too, are sinners under the judgment of death and eternal separation from God. However, there is a way we can live forever with God. Have you received the free gift of salvation? Is your name in the Book of Life? The Holy Scripture warns of a coming judgment. Revelation 20:15 says, "And whosoever was not found written in the book of life was cast into the lake of fire."

If our name is found in the Book of Life, Jesus tells us in John 14:2-3, "In my Father's house are many mansions; if it were not so, I would have told you. I go to prepare a place for you. And if I go and prepare a place for you, I will come again, and receive you unto myself; that where I am, there ye may be also."

We are all sinners. "For all have sinned, and come short of the glory of God" (Rom. 3:23). But Jesus Christ died for sin. "For God so loved the world, that he gave his only begotten Son, that whosoever believeth in him should not perish, but have everlasting life" (John 3:16).

How can you be saved? The Bible says in Romans 10:9, "That if thou shalt confess with thy mouth the Lord Jesus, and shalt believe in thine heart that God hath raised him from the dead, thou shalt be saved." First John 1:9 says, "If we confess our sins, he is faithful and just to forgive us our sins, and to cleanse us from all unrighteousness."

You don't have to be perfect to come to Christ. Read about the thief on the cross (Luke 24:40-43). Jesus Christ will meet you right where you are. "Whosoever therefore shall confess me before men, him will I confess also before my Father which is in heaven" (Matt. 10:32).

If you have confessed your sins and placed your faith in Jesus Christ, you are now a part of the family of God. Please pray, read your Bible daily, and go to a church that teaches the authority of Scripture without compromise (Heb. 10:25). Please call Answers in Genesis and receive a free booklet on what it means to be a Christian (1-800-350-3232).